POETIC INQUIRY AS RESEARCH

Creative Research Methods in Practice

Series Editor: **Helen Kara**, We Research It Ltd.

This dynamic series presents short practical books by and for researchers around the world on how to use creative and innovative research methods from apps to zines. Edited by the leading independent researcher Helen Kara, it is the first series to provide guidance on using creative research methods across all disciplines.

Also available in the series:

- *Sandboxing in Practice* by Dawn Mannay and Victoria Timperley
- *Encountering the World* with I-docs by Ella Harris
- *Doing Phenomenography* by Amanda Taylor-Beswick and Eva Hornung
- *Fiction and Research* by Becky Tipper and Leah Gilman
- *Photovoice Reimagined* by Nicole Brown

Find out more at:
policy.bristoluniversitypress.co.uk/creative-research-methods-in-practice

POETIC INQUIRY AS RESEARCH

A Decolonial Guide

Edited by
Heidi van Rooyen and Raphael d'Abdon

First published in Great Britain in 2025 by

Policy Press, an imprint of
Bristol University Press
University of Bristol
1–9 Old Park Hill
Bristol
BS2 8BB
UK
t: +44 (0)117 374 6645
e: bup-info@bristol.ac.uk

Details of international sales and distribution partners are available at
policy.bristoluniversitypress.co.uk

© Bristol University Press 2025

British Library Cataloguing in Publication Data
A catalogue record for this book is available from the British Library

ISBN 978-1-4473-7323-0 hardcover
ISBN 978-1-4473-7324-7 paperback
ISBN 978-1-4473-7325-4 ePub
ISBN 978-1-4473-7326-1 ePdf

The right of Heidi van Rooyen and Raphael d'Abdon to be identified as editors of this work has been asserted by them in accordance with the Copyright, Designs and Patents Act 1988.

All rights reserved: no part of this publication may be reproduced, stored in a retrieval system, or transmitted in any form or by any means, electronic, mechanical, photocopying, recording, or otherwise without the prior permission of Bristol University Press.

Every reasonable effort has been made to obtain permission to reproduce copyrighted material. If, however, anyone knows of an oversight, please contact the publisher.

The statements and opinions contained within this publication are solely those of the editors and contributors and not of the University of Bristol or Bristol University Press. The University of Bristol and Bristol University Press disclaim responsibility for any injury to persons or property resulting from any material published in this publication.

Bristol University Press and Policy Press work to counter discrimination on grounds of gender, race, disability, age and sexuality.

Cover design: Qube Design
Front cover image: iStock/Veronika Oliinyk

We dedicate this book to our families, who have supported us throughout our journeys as writers. Heidi offers her dedication in loving memory of her sister, Bupsie. Raphael extends his gratitude to his daughter, Atisa, his wife, Nichole, and his parents, Alfonso and Eva.

Contents

List of figures and tables	viii
List of poems	ix
Notes on contributors	xiii
Acknowledgements	xvi
Preface	xviii

1	Embracing poetic inquiry as a decolonial research method *Heidi van Rooyen and Raphael d'Abdon*	1
2	The way of poems *Kirsten Deane, Raphael d'Abdon and Angela Hough*	33
3	Taking poetry into research *Angela Hough, Yvonne Sliep and Heidi van Rooyen*	75
4	Navigating ethical territories in poetic inquiry *Yvonne Sliep, Angela Hough and Duduzile S. Ndlovu*	117
5	Assessing the craft and reach of poetic inquiry *Duduzile S. Ndlovu and Heidi van Rooyen*	155
6	Conclusion *Raphael d'Abdon and Heidi van Rooyen*	183

Index	187

List of figures and tables

Figures

1.1	Heidi van Rooyen's time-map	5
1.2	Key principles for decolonial research	19
2.1	The imaginative power of African languages	40
2.2	'La verre' and 'La bouteille' by Charles-François Panard	54
2.3	Figures of speech	59
3.1	Listening with thin ears	83
3.2	Defining and mapping poetic inquiry	90
3.3	Angela Hough's mind-map	108
4.1	Who does the research serve?	120
4.2	Intersectionality	128
4.3	Multidisciplinarity	136
5.1	Poemish is good enough	158
5.2	Evaluating poetic inquiry	160
5.3	Embracing a decolonial approach	171

Tables

1.1	Key principles and ideas	16
2.1	Afriku examples	42
2.2	Repetition, rhythm and rhyme	66
3.1	Key aspects of poetic inquiry	89
3.2	Exploring trans identities in Namibia: verbatim and poetic transcription	106
5.1	Criteria for evaluating arts-based research	162
5.2	Criteria for evaluating poetic inquiry	165

List of poems

'Whitewash' 3
Nicole Brown and colleagues

'being coloured' 6
Heidi van Rooyen

'decoloniality' 9
Heidi van Rooyen

'This is fine' 15
Reakeeta Smallwood

'Unsilencing my teaching voice' 18
Alexander Timothy

'Found poem: Acceptance' 20
Heidi van Rooyen

'Pass for white' 23
Heidi van Rooyen

'Fathers and Sons' 44
Kirsten Deane

'What you need' 46
Kirsten Deane

'I will remember' 49
Raphael d'Abdon

'Yasmin' 51
James Elroy Flecker

'Can we be like water' 55
Tanya Layne

'Kiliba Village, East DRC' 56
Yvonne Sliep

'Little Pains' 63
Kirsten Deane

'Manifesto of poetic inquiry' 77
Angela Hough

'I am gay' 78
Chammah J. Kaunda and Mathias Alubafi Fubah

'Opening and anchoring' 81
Malika Ndlovu

'The Poet' 82
Angela Hough

'You could scream the place down' 86
Joy

'Home' 87
Zonke Gumede and Monde Makiwane

'shakespeare didn't work for me' 93
Raphael d' Abdon

'Yearning' 96
Makhosazana Xaba

List of poems

'to slam or not to slam?' — 96
Raphael d'Abdon

'In Taiwan' — 99
Yvonne Sliep

'One month' — 100
Yvonne Sliep

'I have no one' — 104
Heidi van Rooyen

'Motherhood' — 107
Angela Hough

'Own my life today' — 122
Duduzile S. Ndlovu

'Less of me' — 130
Yvonne Sliep

'Nobody is safe' — 136
Heidi van Rooyen

'walking the talk is a lifelong process' — 139
Yvonne Sliep

'Belonging begins in exile' — 142
Angela Hough

'The light' — 145
Ingene 'Gene' Corefio Harris

'Bad blood' — 146
Yvonne Sliep

'Re-authoring' 147
Sipho Ngcongo

'How does it sit?' 149
Yvonne Sliep

'This world' 168
Duduzile S. Ndlovu

Notes on contributors

Raphael d'Abdon is a researcher, poet, editor and translator, and a Research Fellow in the Department of English Studies at the University of South Africa. His areas of research are African literature in English, spoken word poetry, decoloniality, poetic inquiry and poetry therapy. His publications include: 'Teaching spoken word poetry as a tool for decolonizing and africanizing the South African curricula and implementing "literocracy"' (2016); 'Transforming data into poems: poetic inquiry practices for social and human sciences' (with Heidi van Rooyen, 2020); 'Carmelo Bene's misreadings of *Hamlet* and *Macbeth*: A decolonial perspective?' (2022); and 'Slam to heal. A poetic inquiry reflection' (2022).

Kirsten Deane is a science writing intern at the Human Sciences Research Council (HSRC). Currently in her first year of a PhD focusing on disability studies, Kirsten aims to empower individuals with disabilities to see themselves positively, challenging societal perceptions. Her poetry has been published both nationally and internationally, and she has spoken at various conferences, including the 8th International Symposium of Poetic Inquiry (ISPI 2022), in Cape Town, and the 28th conference of Performance Studies international (2023), held at the University of the Witwatersrand, where she conducted a poetic inquiry workshop.

Angela Hough is a registered psychologist, therapeutic group facilitator, trainer, process art facilitator, poet, artist and mother of two teenagers. She works in an addiction clinic and has 15 years of teaching experience at the tertiary level in psychology and education at the University of KwaZulu-Natal and the South African College of Applied Psychology. Angela has contributed to scholarly writing on resilience in young people, poetic inquiry, barriers to learning and issues of diversity and decoloniality. She emphasises the importance of enhancing our relational capacities through healing, fostering authentic dialogues and addressing systemic issues with a focus on diversity, inclusion and decolonial practices.

Duduzile S. Ndlovu is a postdoctoral fellow at the University of Johannesburg. She engages in arts-based research methods as a form of decolonising knowledge production. She has written poetry, articles and book chapters on the gendered politics of memory in migrants' cultural productions in Zimbabwean migration to South Africa. Duduzile held a Newton Advanced Fellowship at the University of Edinburgh (2018 to 2020) and edited an open access, self-published text, *Moving Words: Poetry in/as Method*. She completed her PhD at the University of the Witwatersrand, writing on Zimbabwean migrants' use of art (poetry, music, drama, film) to memorialise precarious lives.

Yvonne Sliep is an honorary professor at the University of KwaZulu-Natal's School of Psychology and a research fellow at the Institute for Justice and Reconciliation in South Africa. She is renowned for incorporating creative methodologies through a decolonisation lens in her teaching, research and supervision practices. Yvonne uses poetry as a tool to witness and honour voices in contexts of suffering, silencing and invisibility. Her expertise is in collective healing, social cohesion and the use of narratives in research and practice, areas where she has published extensively.

Heidi van Rooyen is Professor and Chair of the Department of Global Health at the University of Washington in Seattle. Prior to that she worked for 20 years in various senior leadership and executive roles at the HSRC. Her work has focused on community-based and participatory research methods and addresses the intersections of HIV/AIDS and COVID-19 with those outside the mainstream of gender, race, class and sexual orientation. Heidi has been writing and performing poetry for more than a decade. As well as using poetic inquiry in her own research, she has been instrumental in advancing this in various academic institutions in the Global South. She edited two books – *Voices and Silences* (2023, Africa Sun Press) and *Poetic Inquiry for the Social and Human Sciences: Voices from the South and North* (2024, HSRC Press) – that emerged from ISPI 2022.

Acknowledgements

Creating this book was a collaborative effort involving a remarkable group of fellow artists, poets, creatives, poet-researchers and research-poets, all dedicated to harnessing poetry in and for research. We extend our deepest gratitude to our dream team – Angela Hough, Duduzile S. Ndlovu, Kirsten Deane and Yvonne Sliep – who not only conceptualised the curriculum that shaped this book, but also tirelessly developed these ideas into the publication you see today. We look forward to continuing our work together to advance poetic inquiry in the Global South.

We extend our gratitude to the over one hundred participants from Cape Town, Johannesburg and Durban who attended our poetic inquiry workshops. These sessions were enlightening and reinforced our dedication to the transformative and healing potential of poetic inquiry. We are hopeful that these experiences will inspire attendees to further integrate poetic inquiry into their professional practices.

We owe immense gratitude to Marilyn Couch, a research trainee at the Human Sciences Research Council (HSRC), whose diligent, caring and graceful handling of countless administrative and organisational tasks has enriched our collaboration immensely.

Special thanks go to James Durno, a visual artist and graphic harvester of extraordinary talent, who attended all our workshops, listened intently and created images that not only captured but also deepened our discussions on poetic inquiry and its decolonial aims. The selected images in each of the chapters are his doing, and we hope you enjoy them.

We are indebted to the HSRC for their financial support, which enabled the realisation of both the book and the workshops. We could have not done this without Carolina Roscigno and Akhona Mncadi from the HSRC Impact Centre. Their generous,

Acknowledgements

consistent and outstanding support was crucial throughout all phases of this project.

Finally, our heartfelt thanks go to Helen Kara, who discovered our article 'Transforming data into poems' and successfully advocated for its inclusion in the Policy Press imprint by Bristol University Press. We are also immensely grateful to the entire team at Bristol, whose patience, diligence and expertise were instrumental in bringing this book to completion.

Preface

For nearly 30 years, researchers in the humanities and social sciences have been exploring the world and the human experience through poetry. This approach, known as poetic inquiry, has grown globally thanks to events like the International Symposium of Poetic Inquiry (ISPI). The symposium gathers researchers, poets, research-poets and poet-researchers every two years to share ideas and practices, build networks and relationships, enable lively exchanges and advance cross-disciplinary scholarship.

Since starting in 2007, these conferences have been held in the Global North – Canada, the UK and the US. However, the eighth ISPI in May 2022 was a breakthrough hybrid event held in person and online in South Africa. It was the first time the symposium had been held on African soil. A group of research-poets/poet-researchers dedicated to advancing poetic inquiry in the Global South, including the editors and contributors of this book, led the conference. This shift brought fresh perspectives, incorporating rich poetic traditions and Indigenous knowledge systems from the Global South into a field of inquiry that had been shaped by the Global North.

The 2022 symposium theme, 'Intersections of silence and (in)visibility', allowed for a lively and timely dialogue among attendees. It challenged conventional views on what constitutes valid and reliable research evidence and celebrated diverse ways of understanding the world. In a rapidly changing world, reshaped by a decolonisation agenda, more and more researchers and students are seeking research methods that allow them to engage creatively and critically with the 'Euro-Western' ways of knowing being upheld by the academy. This was abundantly evident at ISPI 2022. The event was not just a gathering; it was also a showcase of how poetry and poetic inquiry can challenge and enrich our understanding of complex social issues such as race, class, gender and sexuality and offer ways to disrupt and resist.

South African poet Malika Ndlovu (2023) captures this well in 'Day three', her poetic reflections performed in the closing ceremony.

'Day three'

Masked or unmasked, face to face
Within and outside of sessions
Across continents, in cyberspace
Sharing discoveries, learnings, hurdles
Haunting or freshly surfaced questions
We continue mapping our way together
A luminous web of overlapping conversations.

Inspired by the energy and insights from ISPI 2022, we developed a curriculum and training programme for poetic inquiry as a method for decolonising research. In the two months that followed, we taught 100 academics and poets at various career stages how to engage with poetic inquiry. The feedback was overwhelmingly positive, affirming the power of this approach to breathe new life into research and challenge colonial legacies in academia. The following comments highlight some of this feedback.

- 'I enjoyed different ways of poetic inquiry such as found poetry and generated poetry, and poetic inquiry as a decolonial medium. I resonate with this position, and I want to interrogate the meanings I attach to it.'
- 'The course provided a more in-depth understanding of how poetic inquiry may be used in research. How to include the invisible voice of the researcher and the participants while staying true to the data.'
- 'The decoloniality and reflexivity sessions were among my favourites. The sessions on form allowed for a great recap, while the found poetry session introduced me to a new method.'
- 'I enjoyed learning about different ways of generating and creating poetry. I loved the session, listening differently to the data and then writing. I enjoyed learning about different forms of poetry and the troubling and contesting conventions.'

- 'I enjoyed combining different fields – integration. I enjoyed learning about found poems. It was an incredible surge of information. I enjoyed the questions unanswered, the sense of context, inclusivity and diversity. I enjoyed the combination of artistic expression and skills with data or research-based information.'
- 'I learned about how inquiry exists in poetry itself and how the interconnectedness with poetry may be utilised to enhance representativity. Inquiry is a useful tool or approach for a poet to enrich their poetry.'
- 'I learned about shape poetry. To play around with visual shapes and how various levels can be reinforced by shapes. I learned about art, the art of words, the arts of colour and the art of healing through poetic inquiry.'
- 'I enjoyed learning about ethical considerations when formulating a poem from research data and learning how power dynamics influence research.'

This book is the culmination of a journey that started with ISPI 2022 and threaded into the workshops that followed. It is infused with our experience of more than a decade of teaching, research, education and supervision in poetic inquiry in various institutions in South Africa and beyond. It also draws on our experience as poets, artists and creatives. We do not start on a blank page. We build on a rich foundation laid by previous scholarly and methodological contributions, primarily from the Global North. We are excited to be able to broaden the scope and impact of poetic inquiry by infusing this history with traditions, practices and points of view from the Global South.

Engage with us

Throughout the book, we work with a central framing question: how can poetry in research be a tool to develop and sustain a decolonising project? Whether you are a seasoned researcher or a newcomer curious about the integration of poetry as, and in, research, we hope this book will offer insights and responses to this question. As you read this book, we encourage you not just to absorb information passively but to engage actively with the concepts. Try the exercises, reflect on your own research practices, and consider how poetic inquiry can bring new depth and resonance to your work. Our suggestions and methods are a mere offering. We hope that you will take what resonates, discard what does not and, above all, use the book to develop your skills and craft in poetic inquiry and to find your own way.

Roadmap

This book embarks on a transformative journey through the lens of poetic inquiry, inviting readers to explore the intersection of poetry and academic research as a powerful tool for decolonisation and social justice. Each chapter is designed to build your understanding and application of poetic inquiry progressively as you seek to understand and employ poetic inquiry in your research.

Chapter 1: Embracing poetic inquiry as a decolonial research method

The opening chapter introduces poetic inquiry. It showcases how poetry can transform research by offering fresh insights and by elevating voices often marginalised in academic research. It unpacks the powerful process of decolonisation and how this can radically change the way research is conceptualised and conducted. It describes four key principles to conducting research that is decolonising, and demonstrate that integrating poetry into research can be a powerful catalyst for social justice and change.

Chapter 2: The way of poems

This chapter explores the practical integration of poetry into research, starting with fundamental questions about what poetry is and how it can enrich research. It provides multiple definitions of poetry from poets of diverse backgrounds while emphasising its importance within the Southern African context and its role as a decolonial research method. The chapter also reviews different figures of speech and poetic forms, focusing on the craft of poetry. Through a series of thoughtfully constructed writing techniques and tools, you are invited to engage with poetry whether you are a newcomer or seeking to deepen your existing relationship with it.

Chapter 3: Taking poetry into research

This chapter explores the concept of poetic inquiry in more detail. It outlines four aspects: (1) a decolonial approach to poetic inquiry; (2) the role of poetry in enriching research; (3) found and generated poems; and (4) guidelines for creating research poems. While the chapter emphasises that poetic inquiry can be used at various stages from researcher reflection to exploration of texts and literature to dissemination of research findings, it focuses on practical guidance for crafting poems using data within research contexts. The aim is to spark your curiosity and encourage you to tailor these approaches to your own research needs.

Chapter 4: Navigating ethical territories in poetic inquiry

This chapter addresses the ethical aspects of poetic inquiry, focusing on power, decolonisation and critical reflexivity. It includes exercises to develop reflexivity, increasing the ethical rigour of research. The discussion extends to inclusive representation, visibility of power structures and the use of poetic inquiry for social justice. It challenges conventional mappings of knowledge and encourages a revaluation of whose experiences are highlighted, promoting a deeper exploration of identity through poetry.

Chapter 5: Assessing the craft and reach of poetic inquiry

This chapter addresses the dual perspectives of assessing the quality of poetic inquiry while considering its broader implications for audience engagement. It is rooted in principles from qualitative and arts-based research, emphasising the need for rigorous and aesthetic evaluations that meet both scientific and artistic standards. A critical aspect of this discussion is the decolonial approach to poetic inquiry, which seeks to include marginalised voices and ensure that research outputs are accessible and meaningful across diverse communities.

Chapter 6: Conclusion

The concluding chapter emphasises the transformative power of poetic inquiry as a decolonising tool, integrating indigenous knowledge systems from the Global South into research practice. It advocates using poetry throughout the research process to challenge traditional methods, promote reflexivity and address power dynamics. The chapter also highlights the need for inclusive, audience-centred engagement, positioning poetic inquiry as a vital approach for both creative expression and decolonial research.

Heidi van Rooyen and Raphael d'Abdon
15 May 2024

Reference

Ndlovu, M. (2023) 'Navigation through verse: Part Two: unfolding, being, sharing and closure', in H. van Rooyen (ed), *Voices Unbound: Poems of the Eighth International Symposium on Poetic Inquiry*, Cape Town: Africa Sun Press.

1

Embracing poetic inquiry as a decolonial research method

Heidi van Rooyen and Raphael d'Abdon

Welcome to our book on how to approach poetic inquiry as a decolonising research method. This opening chapter introduces you to poetic inquiry, showcasing how poetry can transform research by offering fresh insights and elevating voices marginalised in academic research. We unpack the powerful process of decolonisation and how it can radically change the way research is conceptualised and conducted. We describe four key principles to conducting research that is decolonising, and we demonstrate that integrating poetry into research can be a powerful catalyst for social justice and change.

Introduction

In recent decades, we have seen a push for more critical and inclusive approaches in qualitative research, challenging conventional academic norms (Denzin, 2017). Some writers, like Davis (2021), argue for qualitative research that allows those who have too often been silenced, made invisible and negatively represented to exist more fully during research. There are many ways that researchers can embrace this goal. Some advocate for more participatory and democratic research practices, others use qualitative research for social justice purposes and yet others try to decolonise research methods (Denzin, 2017).

This turn towards more critical enquiry developed alongside the growing popularity of arts-based research methods (Leavy, 2009, 2015). Poetic inquiry is an umbrella term used to describe the numerous approaches that combine the art of poetry making with the principles of qualitative research (Glesne, 1997; Richardson, 2002; Furman, 2006; Prendergast, 2009). Using poetry in research is not only about adding aesthetic appeal to studies – it also is a profound method to delve into human experiences, bringing them to life vividly and viscerally through and with poetic language. Unlike the conventional research that relies on dense narrative forms, poetic inquiry uses the evocative power of poetry to enhance understanding and empathy, presenting data and insights in a way that resonates deeply with both researchers and participants (Colby and Bodily, 2018).

There is no one way to do poetic inquiry (Prendergast, 2009); the approach allows for a flexible and expressive engagement with research through various integrations of poetry and qualitative methods. It provides a spectrum of integration, from studies dominated by poetic elements to those incorporating subtle poetic touches alongside traditional research components. A remarkable collection of edited books and themed journal issues at the website of the International Symposium of Poetic Inquiry (ISPI; www.poeticinquiry.ca/books-and-collections.html) provides examples that illustrate applications along this spectrum. In our addition to this body of scholarly work, *Poetic Inquiry for the Human and Social Sciences* (van Rooyen and Pithouse-Morgan, 2024), we also illustrate this. In that book, Fezeka Gxwayibeni and Tamuka Maposa use a more traditional qualitative approach infused with poetry to discuss history teachers' engagement with post-apartheid South Africa (Gxwayibeni and Maposa, 2024). Kimberly Dark's piece is centred on five poems that reflect how some bodies, lives and experiences are simultaneously erased and made hyper-visible in the dominant culture (Dark, 2024). Nicole Brown and eight other academics and students provide a dialogic poetic inquiry about their sense of silence and invisibility in the academy (Brown et al, 2024). The extract from one of their poems, 'Whitewash', explores the intersectionality of gender and race.

'Whitewash'

Blank page as confession booth.
Pen as priest.   I confess
I hold the word   white in my mouth,
feel the initial roundness of lips   give way
to tongue on teeth, as if innocent.

If wishing would help,
I'd wish for a world of diverse people,
all equal,   all empowered,   all vital,
I'd wish for a world where my
white,   straight,   able,   middle-class
heart   wasn't the coloniser,
wasn't worn on my sleeve,   bleeding down my arms
to my white hands,   rattling the bars
of my gilded cage   of privilege.
I want to wash the page with wishes
but cannot   erase my power.
Wishes are a whitewash waste of words
that cannot cleanse blood.

Unpacking colonisation

Colonisation describes the control and dominance that Western and European countries have over native and indigenous people around the world (Thambinathan and Kinsella, 2021). The term 'coloniality' refers to the enduring structures and power systems that arose from colonialism. Typically, colonisers, who were mainly White and male, did not just forcibly take land from indigenous people – they also imposed their own ways of thinking and living on the bodies, lives, cultures and selfhoods of original populations they conquered. Colonisation continues to have far-reaching impacts, deeply influencing how indigenous groups continue to see the world and themselves in relation to White, male imperialism (Maldonado-Torres, 2007; Quijano, 2007).

Efforts to question, challenge and change these ingrained ways of thinking and behaving are known as decolonial or anti-colonial movements (Emnet, 2021; Gobena et al, 2023). Crilly and Everitt (2022) describe decolonisation as the process of identifying and confronting colonial systems and relationships. It is not solely about adding non-White cultures' achievements into the mix – it is about a fundamental change in how we understand and balance power in society and how indigenous groups emancipate themselves at all levels (Keele University, 2018, in Crilly and Everitt, 2022).

Fanon (1967) and Maldonado-Torres (2007) highlight the need to critically assess the psychological and societal impacts of colonisation, which have historically positioned colonised peoples as inferior. Decolonisation also requires former colonial powers to critically examine their own cultural beliefs and the ways these beliefs continue to create inequalities among different cultures, classes and genders (Manathunga, et al, 2021).

Time-maps

As researchers interested in doing work that is decolonial, it is important that we wrestle with our colonial history. Manathunga et al (2021) invite us to do a time-map of our colonial history and influences. Time-mapping is a visual methodology that uses art to explore the impact of history, geography, genealogies and cultural knowledge on collective, social, ancestral and traumatic memory. Heidi van Rooyen, one of the authors, describes her ancestral background and history as a mixed-race person in South Africa as follows:

> Apartheid flattened South Africa's complex colonial entanglements and histories into a racial category called coloured. I was designated the label coloured. Coloured has a particular meaning in this part of the world. It does not refer to Black people as it does in Britain and the United States. Coloureds are descendants of the sexual liaisons between colonialists, slaves, the indigenous Khoisan and other groups who settled in the country. Distinct (and distinguished through apartheid law) from the historically dominant white minority and the majority black population, coloureds, as they were mixed blood, were believed to be impure and to carry a number of inbred characteristics because of this. Colouredness has and continues to be associated with negativity, deviance and illegitimacy.

She shows in her time-map (Figure 1.1) how her family's history is shaped by her White, Dutch colonial forefathers who married

Figure 1.1: Heidi van Rooyen's time-map

Black women and how her French Mauritian forefathers found local Indian women when they sailed and settled in South Africa.

> ### Exercise: doing your time-map
>
> We invite you now to draw your own time-map. Trace a path to your connections to colonial oppressions. As you think about the colonial histories and influences in your life, consider the following:
>
> - How have these impacted you, your family and community?
> - What privileges or disadvantages have these historical processes given you?
>
> You could write down your answers to the two questions just posed, either in the form of a journal entry or as a poem.

Over the years, van Rooyen has used poetic inquiry to explore issues such as race, gender, sexuality and identity (van Rooyen, 2019, 2021; Hough and van Rooyen, 2024). The poem 'being coloured' appears in these cited chapters and captures what it felt like, and still feels like, being haunted by Whiteness and seeing Blackness as other.

'being coloured'

being coloured
is to be
outside of whiteness
inside of non-whiteness
outside of Africaness
and blackness

is to live
alongside
the colonial wound
to live
through the wound
by inflicting it

on another Other
is to be
complicit with Apartheid
enamel cups and plates
for the 'girl'
who washes our intimacies
tongues unbothered
to ask her African name

We hope that the exercises in this section give you pause and opportunity to reflect. We believe it is crucial for us to examine our own roles in society and, as researchers, to focus on what influences our perspectives – our subjectivities and positionalities. This includes recognising our privileges and the ways we may face oppression related to race, age, gender, class and other social categories, and understanding how these categories can overlap and intersect. By connecting personally with issues like colonisation, we can better understand how these categories shape our professional work in research and education. This self-awareness enhances our ability to address complexities effectively in our roles as researchers and educators.

Decolonising research

Decolonising research challenges the old ways of thinking about knowledge that favour Western perspectives and claim to be unbiased (Keikelame and Swartz, 2019). This effort aims to develop new ways of understanding and researching that respect and incorporate the views and knowledge of people who historically have been marginalised. It also strives to develop new, inclusive theories and methods that reflect and support the diverse ways of knowing and the perspectives of colonised peoples. Approaches like poetic inquiry not only critique traditional methods but also envision new ways to conduct and understand research.

Scholars from diverse backgrounds, including those focused on postcolonial, feminist and critical theories, lead this change. They critique how knowledge is conventionally produced, suggesting it often promotes a biased understanding of people's experiences, and they advocate for a variety of alternative methods and theories

(Visweswaran, 1994; Denzin, 2003; Denzin and Lincoln, 2003; Cannella and Lincoln, 2004; Mutua and Swadener, 2004). Participatory approaches such as photovoice, autoethnography, visual methods, poetic inquiry and storytelling are just some of the methods used to strengthen decolonisation in research and make research more inclusive (Barnes, 2018).

Linda Tuhiwai Smith's influential *Decolonizing Methodologies* (1999), viewed through an indigenous Maori lens, contends that colonisation infuses research with an 'attitude' and a 'spirit' of ownership over the world. This perspective is reinforced by established systems and governance structures, embedding these beliefs within institutional practices. She suggests that colonial and imperial research approaches convey a sense of innate superiority and an overabundance of desire to bring progress into the lives of indigenous peoples – spiritually, intellectually, socially and economically:

> Research 'through imperial eyes' describes an approach which assumes that Western ideas about the most fundamental things are the only ideas possible to hold, certainly the only rational ideas and the only ideas which can make sense of the world of reality of social life and of human beings. (Smith, 1999, p 6)

Such research 'steals' knowledge for the benefit of those who take it, not those who originally held it (Smith, 1999, p 56).

Bhattacharya (2019) adds that not all research is meant to be imperialist or racist but when it is shaped by Western perspectives and conducted on non-Western subjects, it struggles to fully capture local indigenous realities. This leads to significant gaps in understanding, as the experiences of marginalised peoples are difficult to translate into Western academic narratives (Chow, 1993, in Bhattacharya, 2019). These issues ultimately affect who is recognised as a legitimate researcher and what is considered valid research (Smith, 1999).

These writers have not held back on their views on coloniality and its effects. For change and transformation to occur, such honesty is necessary and important. We acknowledge too, through the words that follow, that discussions on coloniality and decoloniality often trigger most people:

'decoloniality'

decoloniality
not easy to say or hear

decolonising
land   space   knowledge
disciplines   methodologies
selves

defensiveness   discomfort
fear
intrigue impatience
anger arise

let these pages
allow for
contemplative embodied
perspectives
create space for multiple voices
to learn grow
be transformed

Here, we offer you a moment to pause with an exercise designed to help you reflect on and deepen your understanding of colonisation and decoloniality in research. First, please review the box with various definitions of decolonial research.

Definitions of decolonial research

> You should in addition problematise research as a power struggle between researchers and the researched. ... The research you do will have the power to label, name, condemn, describe, or prescribe solutions to challenges in former colonised, indigenous peoples and historically oppressed groups. (Chilisa, 2012, p 25)

> What we know and how we know [are] grounded in shifting and diverse historical human practices, politics, and power. ...

[W]hichever group is strongest establishes its own rules on what can be known and how it can be known. A non-power related truth game is not possible; thus, humanity installs each of its violences in a system of rules and thus proceeds from domination to domination. (Foucault, 1977, p 151)

If a research project does not acknowledge the issues of power relations regarding the context of the research, and the intricate relationship between knowledge and power, this lack of social responsibility renders its technical quality of little significance and its usefulness questionable. (Buskens, 2002, p 5)

Césaire (2001) argues that colonialism at its core is dehumanising and research methodology was born a handmaiden of colonialism and imperialism. (Ndlovu-Gatsheni, 2017, p 187)

Decolonising entails a political and normative ethic and practice of resistance and intentional undoing – unlearning and dismantling unjust practices, assumptions, and institutions – as well as persistent positive action to create and build alternative spaces, networks, and ways of knowing that transcend our epicolonial inheritance. (Kessi et al, 2020, p 1)

Decolonising methodology, therefore, entails unmasking its role and purpose in research. It is also about rebelling against it, shifting the identity of its object to re-position those who have been objects of research into questioners, critics, theorists, knowers, and communicators. (Ndlovu-Gatsheni, 2017, p 188)

Exercise: reflecting on decolonial research practices

Follow the following steps to explore the concepts discussed thus far in the chapter. Doing so will help you consider your own position regarding coloniality and decoloniality.

1. **Review key definitions:** Begin by reviewing the various definitions of decolonial research provided in the box. These definitions have shaped the development of the chapter and provide foundational concepts for decolonial practices.

2. **Select a definition:** Choose one definition that particularly resonates with you. This might be one that you feel best captures the essence of decolonial research or one that challenges your current understanding of research methodologies.

3. **Examine your identity:** Think about the various aspects of your identity – such as your cultural background, education level, gender, race and socioeconomic status – and how these might influence your research perspective. Acknowledging these parts of your identity is crucial for understanding how you interact with and impact the participants in the research you do.

4. **Consider intersectionality:** Explore how different aspects of your identity intersect and how these intersections contribute to your experiences of privilege or marginalisation. Understanding these intersections is essential for adopting a decolonial lens, as this helps to highlight the complexities of power dynamics in research settings.

5. **Write your way into it:** Write down your responses to any or all of these issues. You could develop your answers through free writing or in a journal entry. Poems can often emerge from this kind of free writing. This book, as it unfolds, will provide you with some tools and techniques for writing poems and for using poetry and inquiry to explore complex issues such as colonisation and decolonisation. Perhaps, right at the end, you can return to this page and see if you can take your journal entry or free writing and shape it into a poem or a series of poems on the topic.

Poetic inquiry as a decolonising force

Our approach to poetic inquiry is deeply intertwined with the decolonisation of research. Poetry allows us to see the world through different lenses rather than just in the usual or accepted ways. By using poetry in research, we confront those outdated ways of thinking. By promoting practices rooted in equity, reciprocity and justice, this approach challenges the colonial and patriarchal structures that have historically dominated research (Dutta, 2018). By valuing lived experiences and diverse ways of knowing, poetic inquiry acts as a form of resistance, helping to dismantle oppressive research paradigms. It helps us appreciate complex identities and experiences that cannot easily be summed up with simple labels. This makes poetry a strong ally in striving for social justice, helping to build a foundation of solidarity, reciprocity and fairness in the way we conduct research (Faulkner and Cloud, 2019).

Dutta (2021), like Bhattacharya (2021), argues that poetry is an essential tool for researchers who are committed to addressing real-world issues and changing the status quo. It allows for a deeper engagement with the communities involved, offering a vivid way to express and work through communal and individual struggles. As we use poetry to capture and convey the complexities of human experience, it transforms our understanding and enriches our interactions, paving the way for meaningful changes and new possibilities in research. In the following, van Rooyen explores how poetry and poetic inquiry has been transformative in her life and her work:

> I had been a social scientist for close to a decade when I stumbled upon poetry and poetic inquiry. I used poetic inquiry to inquire into issues of race and identity and to explore the lives of trans women in Namibia and South Africa:
>
> **It felt like coming home.** This bringing together of this creative, expansive poet-self with my day job as a researcher and a scientist. I was now a poet-scientist! Poetic inquiry gave me a new platform to speak to the social justice issues that had shaped my career. Writing

poetry enabled me to 'interrogate the self, within the social and political'.
It awakened me. Over time, we all become dead to our work, and the very issues that we are passionate about. I did too. We find ways to retreat behind the comfort of our position and authority as researchers and knowledge producers. Poetic inquiry forced me to grapple with issues of power, authority and voice as a researcher. There was something about transforming this data into poetry that forced me to acknowledge my own subjectivities, and to write these into text.
It humbled me. The poems brought me closer to the realities of the marginalised lives of trans women in powerful ways. It opened my eyes to the stories of gender and sexual minorities and how these are often lost in endless interview transcripts, in chunks of text, in academic articles never to be seen and read by anyone who matters. These lives were foregrounded, emphasised and distilled in evocative and moving ways in the poems.
It made me human again. Poetry allowed me to fully see these fellow human beings, their stresses and strains, and urged me to become a better collaborator and mediator engaging with and involving participants more fully in my research and in writing.

Bhattacharya (2021) and Dutta (2021) do not believe that poetry offers straightforward answers. However, for those engaged in critical and activist ethnography – a type of research that is based on deep involvement with communities – poetry is tightly linked to real-world experiences and struggles. It becomes a powerful tool for addressing suffering and supporting ongoing efforts to overcome colonial legacies while also exploring the relationships within these communities. This approach allows us to continuously evolve our understanding as our experiences change us.

Throughout this book, we explore how poetic inquiry can serve as a powerful tool for decolonial research. By integrating poetic techniques and approaches, researchers can enhance the expressive power of their work and ensure that it resonates with a wider audience, including those typically excluded from academic discourse. This helps to set the groundwork for using poetic inquiry as a transformative method that not only captures but also respects the richness of diverse experiences and perspectives.

Key principles for decolonial research

The global push for decolonising research aims to rethink the 'Euro-Western' assumptions, motivations and values behind it (Smith, 1999). We have mentioned some of these already, but in the next part of this chapter, we want to expand on several of the principles and practices that shape decolonial research.

Principle 1: Acknowledge and respect indigenous worldviews

Western science often views knowledge through a hierarchical and linear lens, dismissing other forms of knowledge as inferior (Shiva, 1997 and Desai, 2001 in Goduka, 2010). These research traditions continue to dominate, influencing academic practices that diminish and overshadow indigenous worldviews (Goduka, 2010). For Ndlovu-Gatsheni (2017), the privileging of Euro-Western views and epistemology in knowledge production has created a cognitive injustice.

Indigenous knowledge systems, which are integral to communities around the globe, incorporate elements such as poetry into their cultural and intellectual fabric, challenging the notion that Western methods are the only valid forms of science (Khupe and Keane, 2017; Dutta, 2018). Decolonisation continually challenges these prevailing narratives, advocating for the recognition and integration of indigenous methods of, and perspectives on, research. This process not only critiques but also actively dismantles the colonial frameworks that have long suppressed indigenous voices and knowledge (Smith, 1999; Battiste and Henderson, 2000; Dutta, 2018). It emphasises holistic understanding that incorporates body, soul and spirit, recognising that stories, performances and poetry are not merely cultural expressions but pivotal forms of knowledge (Gunner, 2001; Ricard and Veit-Wild, 2005; Finnengan, 2012).

Several South African writers (for example, d'Abdon, 2016, and Bila, 2022) show how decolonial poetry and poetic inquiry can be tools for healing and transformation. d'Abdon (2016) describes spoken word poetry as narrative storytelling that taps into local indigenous knowledge systems and various traditions of oral folklore. In his 2016 poetic inquiry with slam poets, he shows how slam is used in creative, non-linear and liminal ways as a resource to heal colonial wounds and historical and everyday trauma.

Along similar lines, but in an Australian Aboriginal setting, Smallwood (2024) highlights indigenous ways of knowing and broadens the definitions of poetic inquiry to recognise and include these ancestral, local, imaginative and communal modes that have always existed but are often silenced. The closing lines extracted from her poem 'This is fine' capture her work with Aboriginal young people.

'This is fine'

Spread out
Complex to understand
Together
We are all one
Empowered
Know the impact   colonisation   historical trauma
Confident
Having a voice
United
More accepting
Culture
Proud to be Aboriginal
I am Aboriginal   This is fine

Bhattacharya (2021) highlights the importance of decolonising knowledge to address the cognitive injustices perpetuated by predominantly Euro-Western epistemologies. This tries to recognise and elevate indigenous knowledge systems that have been historically marginalised or ignored, fostering a more inclusive and equitable research environment. The decolonisation process is intricate, involving the challenge of normal assumptions about power and identity and the examination of how these elements interact to maintain privilege and inequality. It is not merely

Table 1.1: Key principles and ideas

Key principle	Key idea
1. Acknowledge and respect indigenous worldviews	This principle calls for a significant shift in how knowledge is created and valued, advocating for a research environment where diverse epistemologies are not only acknowledged but are integral to the fabric of global scholarship.
2. Amplify voices from the margins	By shifting from a Eurocentric to a more inclusive approach, decolonial research seeks to dismantle the oppressive structures of knowledge production and place respect, inclusivity and equity at the centre of scholarly inquiry.
3. Foster respectful, collaborative and participatory research	This principle underscores the shift from viewing research subjects as passive data sources to seeing them as active participants in shaping research that directly affects their lives.
4. Embrace critical reflexivity	By recognising and challenging their own positions of power and privilege, researchers can contribute to dismantling the systemic barriers that perpetuate inequality, ensuring their work not only advances knowledge but also promotes justice and equity.

about replacing one form of control with another, nor is it about perpetuating existing power dynamics. Instead, it calls for a 'productive nostalgia', a critical and appreciative re-engagement with indigenous knowledge that helps us reshape our understanding of the future, as discussed by Moletsane (2011, p 206).

By redefining the parameters of academic inquiry to include these rich, often silenced voices, decolonisation fosters a more comprehensive understanding of the world. It enables historically marginalised communities to assert their sovereignty and reshape the research agenda, ensuring that their perspectives are central, not peripheral. This transformation is depicted in the ways indigenous peoples are not only participants in research, but lead as researchers themselves, fundamentally altering how questions are posed and answered. Table 1.1 illustrates the key principles and idea.

Principle 2: Amplify voices from the margins

A decolonial approach requires embracing a wide range of perspectives, especially those of individuals and communities whose existence and experiences have been routinely overlooked or deemed insignificant (Ndlovu-Gatsheni, 2017). Maldonado-Torres (2007) emphasises that decolonisation involves 'making the invisible visible' by examining and dismantling the structures that contribute to this invisibility. This process challenges the dominant knowledge production, which is heavily rooted in the Global North (Zavala, 2013), and strives to disrupt universally accepted notions about human life, providing a platform for those who have been historically marginalised.

Decolonisation is not about discarding all Western methodologies and theories. Rather, it seeks to adapt these frameworks to better fit and benefit local communities (Manathunga et al, 2021).

This requires a fundamental shift from excluding diverse perspectives to embracing and integrating various political philosophies and knowledge systems. Constructive discussions about how conventional knowledge systems can be more inclusive are essential (Melro and Ballantyre, 2022).

It is important to recognise that decolonisation should not merely serve as a metaphor for social justice, but involve tangible changes that respect and prioritise the knowledge and self-determination of indigenous peoples (Chilisa, 2012). When conducting research with indigenous communities, we should place their voices and frameworks of knowledge at the forefront of the research process, valuing their contributions as central rather than peripheral (Smith, 1999).

Indigenous research calls for a reassessment of how academic knowledge is validated and presented, recognising the variety of narratives within colonised and decolonising contexts (Kupe and Keane, 2017; Dutta, 2018). This process involves empowering indigenous communities to lead and reshape the research agenda, significantly altering everything from how questions are formulated to how data is interpreted (Denzin, 2017), presented and disseminated. Additionally, discussions on decolonising methodologies must broaden to include more contributors from the Global South, ensuring that these conversations are not influenced solely by Western perspectives but also encompass a wide array of viewpoints that accurately represent the experiences of those most impacted by colonial histories (Barnes, 2018).

Recent academic contributions, including those presented at ISPI 2022, in this book and in other instances of poetic inquiry in scholarly literature, are fulfilling Barnes's (2018) call for a more inclusive academic discourse. For example, in 'Unsilencing my teaching voice', Alexander Timothy, a Nigerian academic, uses poetic inquiry to question the colonisation of intellectual and academic endeavour in his institution (Timothy and McCreary Sullivan, 2024).

> 'Unsilencing my teaching voice'
>
> *Constructed by civil war,*
> *and rules of the barracks,*
> *I savour the colour of oppression;*
> *nay, its opaqueness.*
> *I dare not verbalise my bonds*
> *nor give verse to my chains.*
> *Yet, I sow my silences in those I tend*
> *cultivating the freedom I covet –*
> *freedom to think and act,*
> *freedom to learn and perform –*
> *that blooms of lights might*
> *harvest the key to my chains*
> *and unlock familial forms of seeking*
> *to know*
> *and be known ...*

Chambers et al (2024) highlight how colonisers' perspectives have influenced the narration, perception and recognition of local stories, histories and truths. This influence is part of a broader pattern of epistemic violence that has silenced, undermined and sometimes completely erased the indigenous knowledge systems of people of African descent. In response, communities have strategically used performance poetry to resist and actively challenge dominant Eurocentric knowledge systems.

Principle 2 underlines the importance of recognising and elevating the voices and perspectives of those who have historically been marginalised within academic and research contexts. By shifting from a Eurocentric to a more inclusive approach, decolonial research seeks to dismantle the oppressive structures of knowledge production and place respect, inclusivity and equity at the centre of scholarly inquiry.

Figure 1.2: Key principles for decolonial research

Principle 3: Foster respectful, collaborative and participatory research

The concept of 'decolonising research' aims to foster equitable and respectful relationships between researchers and community members, ensuring that the knowledge produced is both relevant to and beneficial for the communities involved (Smith, 1999). According to Prior (2010) in Dutta (2018), decolonising research is a process that cultivates meaning through building relationships, trust, reciprocity and collaboratively developed research methods that honour and incorporate indigenous communities' worldviews and cultural values. Figure 1.2 illustrates this process.

Decolonising researchers are tasked with dismantling the typical barriers between themselves and the research participants, addressing emerging ethical concerns as they arise (Kessi et al, 2021). Indigenous scholar Zavala (2013) suggests that decolonisation focuses on creating spaces that amplify indigenous voices and perspectives, which can transform researchers' own identities in the process. This transformative approach calls for engaging with marginalised communities in a manner that is respectful and authentic, employing dynamic methods and ensuring reciprocity throughout the research process (Smith, 1999; Kovach, 2010). By working 'with' rather than 'on' marginalised communities, researchers can help to educate about rights and empower these communities to have a say in how research is conducted and how findings are used (Barnes, 2018).

In their research, South African poet inquirers have shown how effective participatory and collaborative methods are in challenging mainstream authoritative approaches to knowledge production (Pithouse-Morgan et al, 2014; Pillay et al, 2017; van Rooyen et al, 2021). Poetic inquiry engages participants actively in the interpretation, representation and mobilisation of poetry, honouring local voices (Pithouse-Morgan et al, 2014), and this fits well with indigenous ways of knowing and sharing knowledge through relationships and dialogue (Pillay et al, 2017).

van Rooyen et al (2021) highlight a project involving collaborative poetic efforts with trans women in Namibia and South Africa. The project produced ten poems that participants described as empowering. They felt these poems gave voice and visibility to the trans experience – a journey often misunderstood and overlooked. For participants, this was 'the power of the poem'.

'Found poem: Acceptance'

The rest of the world
can do whatever they want,
but this is the point
where you accept you are trans.
You say –
this is what I am.
You stand up
you are trans.
You go to bed
you are trans.
Like literally,
you take a bath
then forget
that whatever you were born with
is of no existence to you.

You get to a point in your life
where you wonder if you ever were a boy.
But if you have a thing in you,

> *you are way past that stage.*
> *Like you don't ever want to go back.*
> *Who would you have been?*
> *You cannot picture yourself as a boy.*
> *It's like you print a thing in your mind.*
> *You wake up like a woman,*
> *do this like a woman.*
> *You feel like a woman,*
> *try so many things like a woman.*
> *You literally sit and think like a woman.*
> *You are a woman.*

Decolonising research seeks to influence both theory and practice by illustrating how indigenous knowledge can be integrated into research outputs, ensuring that findings and recommendations are returned to the indigenous communities for their evaluation and approval. This approach recognises the importance of understanding the social contexts in which people operate, acknowledging that personal experiences, memories and expectations shape how individuals interpret their realities and interact with the world.

Principle 3 emphasises the importance of transforming research practices to be more respectful, collaborative and participatory. By focusing on building genuine relationships with community members and respecting indigenous knowledge systems, researchers can help to ensure that their work not only contributes to academic knowledge but also supports the communities involved. The aim is to create research processes that are inclusive and reflect diverse perspectives, ultimately fostering social justice and reducing inequalities. This principle underscores the shift from viewing research 'subjects' as passive data sources to seeing them as active participants in shaping research that directly affects their lives.

Principle 4: Embrace critical reflexivity

Melro and Ballantyne (2022) define critical consciousness as the 'intentional cultivation of critical reflection that attends to the dynamics of oppression and privilege to identify causes of intergroup inequalities to invoke action' (p 311). The word 'critical' here entails a challenge to the passive acceptance of the status quo and established Euro-Western systems. This is achieved by inquiring into the limitations and contradictions of these systems and beginning to understand how the theories and frameworks that inform them continue to serve inequality and injustice. It is an ongoing process of becoming, unlearning and relearning regarding who we are as researchers and being accountable (Melro and Ballantyne, 2022; Dutta, 2018).

The growing call for decolonisation and self-determination by indigenous scholars and communities alike requires researchers and communities to critically examine their beliefs, assumptions and attitudes within the power and oppression relationship. This requires critical consciousness as to why and how inequities are caused, while also recognising the strength and perseverance to overcome adversity. Such recognition relies on vulnerability and authenticity within the process.

Exercise: thinking about decolonial principles

We have talked in detail about four key concepts that frame a decolonial approach to research. Read back over the principles, then consider and write a response to the following prompts:

1. **Resonance:** Which of the four principles align with your principles and research practice?

2. **Stretching:** Reflect on the principles that felt underdeveloped in your thinking, your processes, your practice. Reflect on how you can incorporate these into your own research practices.

3. **Deepening:** consider specific actions or changes you can make to engage more deeply with a decolonial approach in your projects.

Case study

In a self-reflecting analysis of her own work, Bhattacharya (2009) warns that decolonising research must not perpetuate another set of binaries to justify the critiques it launches. By this, she means that she tries not to be the 'morally and rhetorically victorious voice on the other side of imperialism while dismissing the care and ethical concern with which many researchers work with people in the West' (p 110). She is aware that if she were to do this, she would merely be promoting a counterculture of polarised discourses. This means that she has to work with the messiness of her contradictions and complexities. She has to 'accept [her] white parts, male parts, queer parts, pathological parts, and vulnerable parts' and welcome them all (p 110).

Exercise: reflecting on our messiness

Consider the case study on Bhattacharya (2019), and reflect on the words or sentiments that stood out for you and explain why they struck a chord.

Bhattacharya's introspective analysis sheds light on the importance of working with our contradictions and complications. We are many selves – that is, many competing and contradictory beings. We bring all of these to bear on our research. We do more harm than good if we are blind to this and we fall into polarised language and positions. In 'Pass for white', van Rooyen (2019) reflects on the privilege of her skin colour in her mixed-blood family, and its implications.

'Pass for white'

I looked different.
In a family from charcoal black
to breadcrust brown
sallow yellow and

off-white cream
I could pass for white.
I talked different.
I didn't talk coloured.
I twanged.

Words spilled out
careful and clipped
stripped of blackness
and of home.

That accent helped me
navigate a path
away from the stench
of the oil refinery
that made grannies sick
and left children
with permanent colds.

That twang
gave me safe passage
past the gangsters
shoring up their despair
and sagging jeans
with knives and needles.

But a twang
doesn't cover all your holes.

You can talk like them
move in their circles
buy their homes
drive their cars
but you still leave your family
coughing against pollution
dodging gangsters
running out of hankies
to wipe the kids snotty noses.

At the core of the Bhattacharya case study is an understanding that our identities and our social and political positions significantly influence our interactions with the communities we research. These identities shape our experiences, beliefs and biases, which in turn affect the dynamics of power within research relationships. By becoming critically aware of these dynamics – how different aspects of our identities intersect and interact – we can foster genuine and respectful relationships with community members.

This deeper awareness allows researchers to engage more meaningfully with communities, ensuring that their involvement is not superficial but grounded in a mutual recognition of humanity and shared struggle. Such engagement is crucial for conducting research that is not only ethical but also effective in contributing to real change.

We explore these themes further in Chapter 4, delving into how researchers can continuously reflect on and adjust their approaches to better align with the principles of decolonial and participatory research. This ongoing process of self-reflection and learning is vital for maintaining integrity and relevance in research practices aimed at social justice.

Conclusion

In this opening chapter, we introduced poetic inquiry as a transformative approach that integrates the art of poetry with scholarly research to challenge and redefine conventional academic norms. We explored how this method not only enhances the representation of marginalised voices but also aligns with the principles of decolonisation, and we advocated for a shift towards more inclusive and empathetic research practices. By discussing both the theoretical underpinnings and practical applications of poetic inquiry, we set the foundation for understanding its significant role in promoting social justice and contributing to a more equitable research environment. As we continue, we will delve deeper into the methods, ethics and impacts of poetic inquiry, highlighting its potential to reshape how research is conducted and experienced.

References

Barnes, B.R. (2018) 'Decolonising research methodologies: opportunity and caution', *South African Journal of Psychology*, 48(3): 379–87.

Battiste, M.A. and Henderson, J.Y. (eds) (2000) *Protecting Indigenous Knowledge and Heritage: A Global Challenge*, Saskatoon: Purich.

Bhattacharya, K. (2009) 'Othering research, researching the other: de/colonizing approaches to qualitative inquiry', in J.C. Smart (ed) *Higher Education: Handbook of Theory and Research*, Vol 24, Dordrecht: Springer, pp 105–50.

Bhattacharya, K. (2019) 'Theorizing from the streets: de/colonizing, contemplative, and creative approaches and consideration of quality in arts-based qualitative research', in N.K. Denzin and M.D. Giardina (eds) *Qualitative Enquiry at a Crossroads*, New York: Routledge, pp 109–25.

Bhattacharya, K. (2021) 'Rejecting labels and colonisation: in exile from post-qualitative approaches', *Qualitative Inquiry*, 27(2): 179–84.

Bila, B. (2022, May) 'Poetry and holistic healing: reflecting on Angifi Dladla's Ku Femba as a poetry teaching philosophy for renewal and transformation', [paper presentation], 8th International Symposium on Poetic Inquiry, Cape Town, South Africa.

Brown, N., McAllister, Á., Haggith, M., Buchanan, M., Sikora Katt, E., Kuri, E. et al (2024) 'One in a group: dialogic poetic inquiry into silence and invisibility in the academy', in H. van Rooyen and K. Pithouse-Morgan (eds) *Poetic Inquiry for the Human and Social Sciences: Voices from the South and North*, Cape Town: HSRC Press, pp 187–200.

Buskens, I. (2002) 'Fine lines or strong cords? Who do we think we are and how can we become what we want to be in the quest for quality in qualitative research', *Education as Change*, 6(1): 1–31.

Cannella, G.S. and Lincoln, Y.S. (2004) 'Ethics, research regulations and critical social science', in M. Israel (ed) *Ethics and Politics in Early Childhood Education*, London: Routledge, pp 81–90.

Chambers, L., Gzuha, E., Kwaramba, G., Bailey, R.-A., Mukandoli, C., Pierre-Pierre, V. et al (2024) '"We will not be silenced": using poetic performance to mobilise the stories of African/African-descendant women living with HIV who work in Canadian HIV service work', in H. van Rooyen and K. Pithouse-Morgan (eds) *Poetic Inquiry for the Human and Social Sciences: Voices from the South and North*, Cape Town: HSRC Press, pp 33–50.

Chilisa, B. (2012) *Indigenous Research Methodologies*, London: Sage Publications.

Crilly, J. and Everitt, E. (2022) *Narrative Expansions: Interpreting Decolonisation in Academic Libraries*, London: Facet Publishing.

Colby, S.R. and Bodily, B.H. (2018) 'Poetic possibilities: exploring texts with Ricoeur's hermeneutics', *International Review of Qualitative Research*, 11(2): 162–77.

d'Abdon, R. (2016) 'Teaching spoken word poetry as a tool for decolonizing and africanizing the South African curricula and implementing "literocracy"', *Scrutiny2: Issues in English Studies in Southern Africa*, 21(2), 44–62.

Dark, K. (2024) 'Intersections of silence and (in)visibility – hyper (in)visibility: poems', in H. van Rooyen and K. Pithouse-Morgan (eds) *Poetic Inquiry for the Human and Social Sciences: Voices from the South and North*, Cape Town: HSRC Press, pp 153–64.

Davis, C. (2021) 'Sampling poetry, pedagogy, and protest to build methodology: critical poetic inquiry as culturally relevant method', *Qualitative Inquiry*, 27(1): 114–24.

Denzin, N.K. (2017) 'Critical qualitative inquiry', *Qualitative Inquiry*, 23(1): 8–16.

Denzin, N.K. and Lincoln, Y.S. (2003) *The Strategies of Qualitative Inquiry* (2nd edn), London: Sage Publications.

Dutta, U. (2018) 'Decolonizing "community" in community psychology: towards radical relationality and resistance', in S. Kessi, S. Suffla and M. Seedat (eds) *Decolonial Enactments in Community Psychology*, New York: Springer, pp 272–82.

Dutta, U. (2021) 'The politics and poetics of "fieldnotes": decolonizing ethnographic knowing', *Qualitative Inquiry*, 27(5): 598–607.

Emnet, T.W. (2021) 'Decolonising a higher education system which has never been colonised', *Educational Philosophy and Theory*, 53(9): 894–906.

Fanon, F. (1967) *A Dying Colonialism*, New York: Grove Press.

Faulkner, S.L. and Cloud, A. (2019) *Poetic Inquiry as Social Justice and Political Response*, Wilmington, DE: Vernon Press.

Finnengan, R. (2012) *Oral Literature in Africa*, Cambridge: Open Book Publishers.

Foucault, M. (1977) *Discipline and Punish: The Birth of the Prison* (trans A. Sheridan), New York: Random House.

Furman, R. (2006) 'Poetic forms and structures in qualitative health research', *Qualitative Health Research*, 16(4): 560–66.

Glesne, C. (1997) 'That rare feeling: re-presenting research through poetic transcription', *Qualitative Inquiry*, 3(2): 202–21.

Gobena, E.B., Hean, S., Heaslip, V. and Studsrød, I. (2023) 'The challenge of western-influenced notions of knowledge and research training: lessons for decolonizing the research process and researcher education', *Journal of Ethnic and Cultural Diversity in Social Work*. doi:10.1080/15313204.2023.2197272

Goduka, N. (2010) 'A framework for decolonising research methodologies', *Calabash: Indigenous Studies Journal*, 4: 73–82.

Gunner, L. (ed) (2001) *Politics and Performance: Theatre, Poetry and Song in Southern Africa*, Johannesburg: Witwatersrand University Press.

Gxwayibeni, F.C. and Maposa, T.M. (2024). 'The captured-uncaptured: learning about millennial history teachers' engagement with post-apartheid South Africa through poetic inquiry', in H. van Rooyen and K. Pithouse-Morgan (eds) *Poetic Inquiry for the Human and Social Sciences: Voices from the South and North*, Cape Town: HSRC Press, pp 245–54.

Hough, A. and van Rooyen, H. (2024) 'Giving voice through love: an ethnographic poetic inquiry', in H. van Rooyen and K. Pithouse-Morgan (eds) *Poetic Inquiry for the Human and Social Sciences: Voices from the South and North*, Cape Town: HSRC Press, pp 15–31.

Keikelame, M.J. and Swartz, L. (2019) 'Decolonising research methodologies: lessons from a qualitative research project, Cape Town, South Africa', *Global Health Action*, 12(1): art 1561175. doi: 10.1080/16549716.2018.1561175.

Kessi, S., Marks, Z. and Ramugondo, E. (2020) 'Decolonizing African studies', *Critical African Studies*, 12(3): 271–82.

Kessi, S., Boonzaier, F. and Gekeler, B.S. (2021) 'Pan-Africanism and psychology: resistance, liberation, and decoloniality', in *Pan-Africanism and Psychology in Decolonial Times*, Cham, Switzerland: Palgrave Macmillan, pp 1–20.

Khupe, C. and Keane, M. (2017) 'Towards an African education research methodology: decolonising new knowledge', *Educational Research for Social Change*, 6(1): 25–37.

Kovach, M. (2010) 'Conversation method in indigenous research', *First Peoples Child and Family Review*, 5(1): 40–8.

Leavy, P. (2009/2015) *Method Meets Art: Arts-Based Research Practice*, New York: Guilford Press.

Maldonado-Torres, N. (2007) 'On the coloniality of being: contributions to the development of a concept', *Cultural Studies*, 21(2–3): 240–70.

Manathunga, C., Qi, J., Bunda, T. and Singh, M. (2021) 'Time mapping: charting transcultural and First Nations histories and geographies in doctoral education', *Discourse: Studies in the Cultural Politics of Education*, 42(2): 215–33.

Melro, C.M. and Ballantyne, C.T. (2022) 'Decolonising community-based participatory research: applying arts-based methods to transformative learning spaces', in P. Liamputtong (ed) *Handbook of Qualitative Cross-Cultural Methods*, Cheltenham: Edward Elgar, pp 309–23.

Moletsane, R. (2011) 'Culture, nostalgia, and sexuality education in the age of AIDS in South Africa', in C. Mitchell, T. Strong-Wilson, K. Pithouse and S. Allnutt (eds) *Memory and Pedagogy*, London: Routledge, pp 193–208.

Mutua, K. and Swadener, B.B. (eds) (2004) *Decolonizing Research in Cross-Cultural Contexts: Critical Personal Narratives*, Albany: State University of New York Press.

Ndlovu-Gatsheni, S. (2017) 'Decolonising research methodology must include undoing its dirty history', *Journal of Public Administration*, 52(S1): 186–8.

Pillay, D., Pithouse-Morgan, K. and Naicker, I. (2017) 'Self-knowledge creation through collective poetic inquiry: cultivating productive resistance as university academics', *Cultural Studies ↔ Critical Methodologies*, 17(3): 262–5.

Pithouse-Morgan, K., Naicker, I., Chikoko, V., Pillay, D., Morojele, P. and Hlao, T. (2014) 'Entering an ambiguous space: evoking polyvocality in educational research through collective poetic inquiry', *Perspectives in Education*, 32(4): 149–70.

Prendergast, M. (2009) 'The phenomena of poetry in research: "Poem is what?" Poetic inquiry in social science research', in M. Prendergast, C. Leggo and P. Sameshima (eds) *Poetic Inquiry*, Boston: Sense Publishers, pp xix–xlii.

Quijano, A. (2007) 'Coloniality and modernity/rationality', *Cultural Studies*, 21(2–3): 168–78.

Ricard, A. and Veit-Wild, F. (eds) (2005) *Interfaces Between the Oral and the Written, Interfaces entre l'écrit et l'oral*, Leiden: Rodopi.

Richardson, L.W. (2002) 'Poetic representations of interviews', in J.F. Gubrium and J.A. Holstein (eds) *Handbook of Interview Research: Context and Method*, London: Sage Publications, pp 877–92.

Smallwood, R. (2024) 'Historical trauma and resilience: Finding Poetics to amplify Australian Aboriginal young people's voices', in H. van Rooyen and K. Pithouse-Morgan (eds) *Poetic Inquiry for the Human and Social Sciences: Voices from the South and North*, Cape Town: HSRC Press, pp 63–76.

Smith, L.T. (1999) *Decolonizing Methodologies: Research and Indigenous Peoples*, London: Zed Books.

Thambinathan, V. and Kinsella, E.A. (2021) 'Decolonizing methodologies in qualitative research: creating spaces for transformative praxis', *International Journal of Qualitative Methods*, 20. doi: 10.1177/16094069211014766

Timothy, A. and McCrary Sullivan, A. (2024) 'Unsilencing: poetic inquiry as an act of resistance in the University of Calabar, Nigeria', in H. van Rooyen and K. Pithouse-Morgan (eds) *Poetic Inquiry for the Human and Social Sciences: Voices from the South and North*, Cape Town: HSRC Press, pp 77–88.

van Rooyen, H. (2019) 'Race and identity in post-apartheid South Africa: making Colouredness visible through poetic inquiry', in S. Faulkner and A. Cloud (eds) *Poetic Inquiry as Social Justice and Political Response*, Wilmington, DE: Vernon Press, pp 87–97.

van Rooyen, H. (2021) 'The race for Colouredness in contemporary South Africa', in R.E. Rinehart, J. Kidd and K.N. Barbour (eds) *Ethnographic Borders and Boundaries*, Bern, Switzerland: Peter Lang UK, pp 77–87.

van Rooyen, H. and Pithouse-Morgan, K. (eds) (2024) *Poetic Inquiry for the Human and Social Sciences: Voices from the South and North*, Cape Town: HSRC Press.

van Rooyen, H., Essack, Z., Mahali, A., Groenewald, C. and Solomons, A. (2021) '"The power of the poem": using poetic inquiry to explore trans-identities in Namibia', *Arts and Health*, 13(3): 315–28.

Zavala, M. (2013) 'What do we mean by decolonizing research strategies? Lessons from decolonizing, indigenous research projects in New Zealand and Latin America', *Decolonization: Indigeneity, Education and Society*, 2(1): 55–71.

2

The way of poems

Kirsten Deane, Raphael d'Abdon and Angela Hough

> This chapter explores the practical integration of poetry into research, starting with fundamental questions about what poetry is and how it can enrich research. It provides multiple definitions of poetry from poets of diverse backgrounds, while emphasising its importance within the Southern African context and its role as a decolonial research method. This chapter also reviews different figures of speech and poetic forms, focusing on the craft of poetry. It invites you, through a series of thoughtfully constructed writing techniques and tools, to engage with poetry as a newcomer or to deepen your existing relationship with it.

Introduction

This book explores the use of poetic inquiry within the social and human sciences, starting with an essential inquiry: what is poetry?

For centuries, humans have used storytelling, enactment, dance, songs and poems to make sense of and tell others about their experiences, feelings, events and lives. Poetry uses words and rhythm to capture experiences, striving to distil images or moments into expressive language, often capturing beauty, posing questions and embracing contradictions. Josep Almudéver Chanzà (2021, p 1) describes poetry as a 'reflex and reflective practice' conducive to meditation, expression and, ultimately, spiritual self-care. Poetry makes the authors' experiences visible and available for readers to engage with. A poem inherently reflects the writer's position. It may be a tool to spark conversations and reflect on intersectional identities and experiences. Poems also have the potential to untangle binaries by making explicit life's paradoxes and juxtapositions (Almudéver Chanzà, 2021).

Poetry thus fosters empathy and insight, giving voice to feelings, experiences and moments that are deeply personal and, in doing so, making them shareable. By allowing marginalised experiences to be heard, poetry can lay the groundwork for change and build bridges over our doubts, curiosities and fears.

Next, we invite you to reflect on what poetry means to you.

Exercise: discovering definitions of poetry

1. Refer to the definitions of poetry listed here. You might also search for other definitions.
2. Choose one definition (or more) that resonates with you. Consider why this definition speaks to you more than others.

Definitions of poetry:

> Poetry is words that are empowered, that make your hair stand on end, that you recognize instantly as being some form of subjective truth that has an objective reality to it because somebody has realized it. – Allen Ginsberg. (in *No Direction Home: Bob Dylan*, 2005)

> Poetry is a diary kept by a sea creature who lives on land and wishes he could fly. – Carl Sandburg

> [N]ot to transmit thought but to set up in the reader's sense a vibration corresponding to what was felt by the writer is the peculiar function of poetry. – A.E. Housman

> Poetry is the language in which man explores his own amazement. – Christopher Fry

> Poetry is a rhythmical form of words which express an imaginative-emotional-intellectual experience of the writer's … in such a way that it creates a similar experience in the mind of his reader or listener. – Clive Sansom

> Poetry is thoughts that breathe, and words that burn. – Thomas Gray

> Poetry heals the wounds inflicted by reason. – Novalis
>
> Poetry is a distillation of the universe. That's what it is. When we attempt to let our time on this planet, and [that] of those who came before us on this planet come together on the tip of a ballpoint pen and explode on the page. That for me is poetry. – Lesego Rampolokeng (in Keylock, 2014)
>
> [P]oems are stories. Poems are stories that reflect the human experience. And the best poetry expresses or mirrors the relationship between a human being and the forces that surround his or her life. – Lance Henson

Poetry lies at the core of poetic inquiry. To become a poet-researcher or researcher-poet, you must strengthen your poetry skills, a theme we revisit throughout this book. You can start with reading poetry, as this can significantly enhance your understanding. You will learn even more writing your own poems. The following exercise is designed to help you engage with and create poetry.

> ### Exercise: connect with a poem
>
> 1. Choose a poem that speaks to a personal experience. This can be any type of poem – slam poetry, song lyrics, classical poetry or poetry from your cultural background, in your native language, either in a formal or informal style.
>
> 2. Write a sentence explaining why this particular poem resonates with you. What in it reflects your own experiences or feelings?
>
> 3. Craft a response to the poem in your own words. This could be a reflection, another poem or a short piece

> of prose expressing how the poem speaks to you or enhances your understanding of your experience.

Everyone brings their own unique experiences and perceptions of poetry to poetic inquiry, and these can vary greatly. As you begin this exploration, you may find it useful to revisit some of your earlier experiences with poetry, as they could shape how you now engage with poetry in research.

> ## Exercise: exploring your relationship with poetry
>
> 1. Think back to your experiences with poetry, both in educational settings and in your personal life. Reflect on both the positive and negative aspects. Consider emotions such as creativity or challenges – for instance, the feeling that you cannot write poetry. Evaluate these thoughts.
>
> 2. Write a brief paragraph about these experiences. Describe specific events that have influenced your perspective, and explain how these experiences have shaped your feelings towards poetry.

We now shift the focus to key techniques, such as poetic forms and figures of speech. Accompanied by practical exercises, these discussions aim to significantly improve your poetry skills.

Poetry as an indigenous knowledge system

What connects diverse indigenous groups such as the Anishinaabe (Gross, 2016) and the Dinè (Klara and Harris, 2019) of North America, the Mayans (Hull, 2016) and Mapuche (Sequeira, 2023) of South America, the Basque (White, 2003) and Sardinians (Zedda, 2009) of Europe, the Mongolians (Chao, 1997) and Siberians (Hatto, 2017) of Asia, the Maori (McRae, 2017) and

Aboriginal (Clunies, 1986) peoples of Oceania, and the Berber (Webber, 2008) and Vatsonga (Mahungana, 1999) peoples of Africa? Despite their geographical differences, these communities share a rich heritage of millennia-old oral cultures and traditions where poetry is central to their indigenous knowledge systems.

The importance of sharing knowledge through oral traditions and poetry – not relying on written texts – is well established in scholarly research and illustrated by the legendary storyteller Shahrazad in *The Thousand and One Nights* (Otiono, 2021, offers a brilliant analysis of this classic text). Shahrazad is noted for her extensive knowledge acquired through stories and poetry: 'Shahrazad ... had read various books of histories, and the lives of preceding kings, and stories of past generations: it is asserted that she had collected together a thousand books of histories relating to preceding generations and kings, and works of poets' (Eliot, 1937, p 10).

To truly pursue a decolonial agenda within both academic and practical realms, it is crucial to study, absorb, preserve, archive and integrate this rich global heritage of oral histories, poetry and indigenous knowledge into current and future research practices. Doing so will reaffirm and enhance poetry's role as a legitimate and indispensable system of knowledge, underlining its significance as a decolonial research methodology.

Poetry in Africa

Reflecting on extensive literature, van Rooyen and d'Abdon (2020, p 13) highlight the integral role of poetry in Africa as a primary means for passing down knowledge across generations. They state that 'poetry is scholarship and, as such, is located at the very centre of the ceremonial cultures of the indigenous people of Africa, of their rituals, and cultural, educational, and social practices'. Building on this foundation and historical insights, they advocate for poetic inquiry as an appropriate research method for those involved in decolonial theory and practice.

This perspective is supported by Chambers et al (2024, p 13), who describe poetic inquiry as an Afrocentric 'home knowing'; they say: 'Poetry as a method of inquiry has been embraced by peoples of African descent because of its congruence with Afrocentric approaches to knowledge gathering and sharing.'

Furthermore, they emphasise that poetry is seen as an inherently Afrocentric art form that existed long before and beyond European colonisation. Harry Garuba (2003, p 609) asserts that 'of the three major genres of literature – drama, the novel, and poetry – it is only poetry that has always been universally accepted by scholars and critics as being indigenous to Africa.'

Audre Lorde also recognises poetry as a vital conduit for consciousness for peoples of African descent, offering a way to reconnect with pre-colonial ways of knowing (Chambers et al, 2024, pp 34–5).

Poetry in Southern Africa

Poetry is deeply embedded in the 'collective genius' of South African people (Kgositsile, nd). It has a crucial role in shaping the South African imagination and is a fundamental part of everyday rituals and practices across communities. This region, home to the earliest-known human ancestors, has a rich history that has been poetically documented by indigenous groups such as the Khoi, San, Xhosa, Zulu, Swazi and Basotho, among others (Vilakazi, 1945, 1993; Kunene M., 1961; Finnegan, 1970; Kunene, D.P., 1971; Dhlomo, 1977; Opland, 1983, 1998; Okpewho, 1990; Hofmeyer, 1993; Kaschula, 1993, 2002; Gunner, 1994; Brown, 1998, 2006; Krog, 2004; Sone, 2011; Maimane and Mathonsi, 2021).

South Africa recognises 11 official languages, including 9 of African origin and 2 of European origin (Afrikaans[1] and English), along with numerous other indigenous languages, dialects and lingos. These indigenous languages are richly figurative, inventive and imaginative – essentially, poetic. Despite the impacts of colonialism, apartheid and neocolonialism, the traditions and languages of South Africa's indigenous people have endured and, as Phakathi (2021) points out, the lessons from these languages remain pertinent and valuable today.

The imaginative power of African languages

In an article for the online South African poetry magazine *Poetry Potion*, Phakathi (2021) shares three anecdotes that illustrate

Figure 2.1: The imaginative power of African languages

the imaginative power of African languages, showcasing their inherently poetic nature.

In the first story, an enraged mother addresses her daughter, who planned to move in with her boyfriend, saying: 'Ha otswa ka lemati leno, o siye sohle seleng saka, le madi atabohang mmeleng ono wahao.' A prosaic rendition of this statement would be 'I will disown you if you walk out that door.' However, the direct translation is: 'At your exit, cast behind all my belongings, even the blood that tears through that body of yours.'

The second story spotlights a man who borrows money from a friend and reassures him by saying: 'Ke molora fela nou Ntjamme, mara oskashwa, sbandaba bhoda rea tsoha.' This could be paraphrased as: 'I'm broke brother, but rest assured, I'll have money at the end of the month.' The actual translation (illustrated in Figure 2.1) is another example of sublime poetic expression: 'All I am now is only but ash my kin; die not, however, when the cold is deemed departed, we shall rise.'

In the final story, Phakathi explains how in certain parts of South Africa, the end of the month is called *sbandana bhoda* or 'the death of the cold'. 'Death' is referred to as *bhoda*, derived from the English word 'border', denoting a crossing over or departure. In other words, when people get paid, the discomfort (cold) that comes from a lack of money departs, even if it's only for a moment.

Using these examples, Phakathi discusses the essence of poetry, recalling the Greek root *poesis*, which means 'the activity in which a person brings something into being that did not exist before'. He concludes that poetry is an art form that uses language to vividly convey ideas, employing poetic devices as instruments to create a powerful sensory impression. As Aimé Césaire succinctly puts it, the essence of poetry is to 're-establish a personal, fresh, compelling, magical contact with things' (Phakathi, 2021).

> **Case study: Afriku, an Africanised poetic form**
>
> 'Afriku', or African haiku, is a term coined by late Ghanaian poet and scholar Adjei Agyei-Baah, the co-founder of Africa Haiku Network and the journal *Mamba*, the leading publication on haiku in the African continent. African *haijin* (haiku poets) use the traditional elements of the ancient Japanese form to create African-centred haiku and tell African stories, thus Africanising one of the oldest and most popular poetic forms in the world. Three examples of afriku are shown in Table 2.1.

We provide an exercise on haikus. However, before you start, there are two things to be aware of.

First, you must know the basic elements of haiku, which is that they:

- **Don't have a title:** Titles are explanatory and, when added, they compromise the intrinsic 'openness' of the form.
- **Rely on brevity:** Haiku take the principle of economy of words to the ultimate level by focusing on one or two images. In English, images are often separated with a dash or other punctuation.
- **Build on fragmentary grammar:** In haiku, adjectives, auxiliary verbs, adverbs and articles are omitted, thus disrupting conventional English grammar.

Table 2.1: Afriku examples

Afriku	Author
farmer's market the scent of melon trails me home	Celestine Nudanu (Ghana)
black mamba coiled in sugar cane field scythe glistening	Raphael d'Abdon (South Africa)
wind storm a tree a possessed priest	Kariuky Wa Nyamu (Kenya)

- **Create a backdrop against which an action takes place:** This could improve use of *renso*, or association of ideas. Static and dynamic images ('fragment' versus 'phase') are juxtaposed to create an 'internal comparison' of ideas.
- **Don't use rhyming:** Rhymes make haiku intolerably monotonous and are systematically avoided.
- **Create a connection with nature:** Haiku habitually include a *kigo*, a word taken from the natural world that sets the poem in a particular season (for example, cherry blossoms).
- **Describe a single, small event in the present tense:** This is the 'haiku moment' – attention is placed on ordinary, delicate objects over the spectacular and sublime.
- **Invest in sensuous details:** Emotions, when they are mentioned directly, are not dwelled on, but stated plainly and directly.
- **Signal the focus early on:** Give a clear-cut picture of a high moment that serves as a starting point for a train of thought and emotion.
- **Rely on the power of suggestion:** Haiku do not put words 'between the truth and ourselves'. The images are filled with overtones that allow the reader or listener to imagine an entire scene, or even multiple scenes.
- **Go in-depth:** The emphasis on unadorned immediacy (*shasei*) and sensory imagery allows the reader to sense a deeper meaning. Images are often symbols of universal themes (life, death, birth and rebirth, interconnectedness, love, sorrow and

so on), and the poems reverberate universal emotions (joy, stupor, melancholy and even despair). The most accomplished haiku can evoke an entire way of life.

Second, *forget about 5-7-5!*
Commonly, and erroneously, haiku written in English follow a structure of 5-7-5 syllables, but in Japanese they are usually written in a single line that can be broken into five, seven and five *sound units* (not syllables). The vast majority of translators, linguists, scholars and leading haikuists maintain that about 10 to 14 English syllables is approximately equal to the 17 sounds they count in Japanese haiku (and, in any case, not all haiku in Japanese have 17 sounds). Therefore, a 17-syllable English poem encloses significantly more content than a 17-sound Japanese poem. In light of this, it is generally accepted that writing 5-7-5 syllable haiku in English is a *violation* of the original form rather than a preservation of it.

In the exercise therefore, do not focus on the 5-7-5 syllabic scheme that you might have learned, but rather on the elements just listed.

Exercise: write an afriku

1. Choose one (or more) afriku from those included in Table 2.1 and write an afriku in response.
2. Your afriku must have the same setting as the one you chose (a market, a field, a storm).

Now it's time to write.

Poetic forms

The preceding section paved the way to for a discussion on various poetic forms, each rooted in distinct cultural or traditional backgrounds. As we saw with afriku, poetic forms may be used in their traditional styles or adapted for contemporary poetry. The examples explored in this chapter are **free verse, narrative poems, golden shovel poems, ghazals, shape poems** and **pantoum**.

Poetic forms provide specific structures that improve rhythm, musicality and conciseness, offering a broader perspective. Each form typically follows a set of rules that shape the poem. It is crucial to understand that all poems have a form, even those written in free verse. We begin this exploration by sharing a free verse poem written by one of the contributors of this chapter, Kirsten Deane.

Free verse

'Fathers and Sons'

They're like nothing else
not like dogs but lions
who hunt in the same hunting ground

They hunch down
they are boneless babies
and they eye the springbok.

They take turns
one for you, another
for your sister

bursting forth
fast and flawless
they grab you by your neck

teeth first
and then claws all in your throat
Then they wait

For you to cry
helping you up
once you have bled enough.

Free verse poetry does not adhere to any strict rhyming or rhythmic patterns, providing poets with the freedom to explore various structures. Though without traditional rhyme and rhythm, free verse poetry uses literary techniques to strengthen its effect. In free verse, each line, stanza and phrase can follow its own distinct flow. Rhythm and musicality are crafted through pauses, breaks and 'silences' rather than the fixed meters found in other poetry forms. Free verse aims to mimic natural human speech and often reads as if it is in direct conversation with the reader. It paints vivid images, allowing readers to navigate the narrative using their own imagination and visualisation skills. Additionally, free verse is known for its rhythmic improvisations, similar to those in jazz music, which add a dynamic quality to the poetry.

Exercise: crafting flow and rhythm in poetry

1. **Create natural flow:** Write two lines that flow smoothly without using any punctuation. Begin the first line with 'they prefer' and the second line with 'they survive'. Each line should make sense independently, and one should complement the other when read together.

2. **Introduce rhythmic variation:** Compose two lines that alter the rhythm of your poem. Use vivid imagery and unconventional line breaks to help the reader visualise the scenes you depict.

Narrative poems

Narrative poems blend the art of storytelling with poetic techniques, functioning much like 'poetic short stories'. They incorporate plots into poetry, enriching the narrative with both literary and poetic methods. Key characteristics of narrative poems include:

1. **Storytelling emphasis:** Narrative poems are built around well-defined characters, plots, settings, actions, climaxes and resolutions. They also employ poetic techniques such as meter, rhythm and various poetic devices to enhance the storytelling.
2. **Experimental language:** These poems often feature unexpected and innovative word choices and diction that aim to surprise, delight, awe, transfix, move, inspire and captivate readers.

3. **Non-linear story structure:** Rather than following a straightforward, chronological narrative, narrative poems may jump back and forth in time, begin in the middle of the story or interweave separate events before merging them into a cohesive whole.

The following is an example of a narrative poem, also by Kirsten Deane:

'What you need'

When you come home from work
the kettle has to be freshly boiled
steaming enough to kill the miggies that fly in through the
kitchen window
a good test for your wife's cleanliness
(Cleanliness is next to Godliness)

The windows should be closed and locked
the cold must be shut out and your children
should be sleepy enough not to bother you
(You should always respect your parents)

The curtains need to be closed
the neighbours can't be trusted when you have a wife
you have to live in the dark
you say that men always get what they want like spiders
crawling out of the shower drains

The shower drains have to be blocked by hand
(Water should never be wasted)
You say your children will never know gratitude
until their skins are dry and falling off the bone

You often think about your life as a child
(How your skin was always brown and the dirt
didn't matter)
You often wish you could come home to yourself
instead.

Exercise: creating a character for a narrative poem

This exercise is designed to help you develop a character for a narrative poem. We will revisit and refine this character throughout this section. Follow the following prompts to build a detailed character profile:

1. Character development

- **Identity:** Who is your character? Give their name and age, and describe their appearance.
- **Background:** Where do they live? What is the cultural setting? Describe their personal history, such as educational background.
- **Personality and motivation:** What are their key personality traits? What drives them in life? What are their fears and ambitions?
- **Relationships:** Describe the relationships they have with others, which could include family, friends, adversaries or love interests.

2. Character needs

- Using detailed imagery, write three to four lines that vividly illustrate what your character needs. These needs could be emotional, physical or spiritual, and they should be integral to their role in the poem.

3. Character dialogue

- Compose two to three lines of dialogue that express your character's internal thoughts or show what they would say in a conversation with another character. This

> dialogue should provide insight into their reasoning, conflicts and desires.

By detailing these aspects of your character, you will create a solid foundation for them within your narrative poem, making them resonate more deeply with readers.

In Chapter 3, we examine found and generated poems within the context of research. Found poetry involves collecting text from diverse sources – such as articles, speeches, letters and other poems – and rearranging these pieces to form a new poem. In the paragraphs that follow, we present a peculiar expression of a found poem, known as 'golden shovel'.

Golden shovel poetry

Golden shovel poetry is a new form named after a poem written by African-American poet Terrance Hayes (see Hayes, 2010, pp 6–8) and popularised by Jericho Brown (2020, p 108) among others. Hayes's 'The golden shovel' uses Gwendolyn Brooks's (nd) 'We real cool' as a source poem,[2] and Brown celebrates the same 'matriarchive' (Phalafala, 2024) in his golden shovel poem 'Stay', developed after Brooks's line 'It was restful, learning nothing necessary'.

The golden shovel expands on forms like the cento and erasure (Brewer, 2014) by offering more creative flexibility than other types of found poems; as explained by Bintz (2023, p 30):

> The purpose of golden shovel poetry is to inspire the writing of other poems. It is a poetic format that uses words from an existing poem to create a new poem. This format invites authors to borrow a line, or lines, from an original poem and use each of the words as the end-words to create a new poem.

Here is how to write one:

1. Select a line or lines from a poem you admire.
2. Use each word from the chosen line(s) as the final word of each line in your new poem.

3. Keep the ending words in the same order as they appear in the original text.
   Also:
4. Acknowledge the poet whose line(s) you are using.
5. The subject of your new poem does not need to match the theme of the original work.

The length of your poem is determined by the number of words in the line or stanza you select: for example, choosing a line with six words will yield a six-line poem, while a stanza with 24 words will produce a 24-line poem.

Next is the golden shovel poem 'I will remember' written by d'Abdon after lines taken from Maya Angelou's (nd) poem 'Kin':

> 'I will remember'
>
> *in the space where you ebbs into we,* ***i***
> *sensed intense vibrations, and i* ***will***
> *always, always* ***remember***
> *your love, fierce yet* ***silent***,
> *like wild horses accustomed to* ***walks***
> *towards the horizon* ***in***
> *fields reddened by a* ***southern***
> *sun, yellowed by northern* ***woods***
> *their steps sure, soft* ***and***
> *slow, echoing, where the* ***long***
> *river cutting the land loose* ***talks***
> *to travelers who stop to listen* ***in***
> *pensive moods, their eyelids* ***low***,
> *as if staring into nearby* ***voices***

Exercise: crafting a golden shovel poem

Having explored what a golden shovel poem entails, along with an example, we encourage you to create one of your own. You could select one of the lines of poetry to construct your golden shovel poem:

Living on autopilot
the days just get away
notice the swirl
put down the knife
great abundance awaits (Heidi van Rooyen)

Sleep my little man-child,
Daylight has gone.
There's no twitter in the branches,
Dream-time has come (Bertrand N.O. Walker, nd)

at the centre of the margins
a quiet view
of places left
and paths imagined (Raphael d'Abdon, 2013, p 23)

Ghazal

The ghazal[3] is a poetic form steeped in themes of melancholy, love, longing and metaphysical contemplation. It originated in 7th-century Arabia and rose to prominence in the 13th and 14th centuries through the works of Rumi and Hafiz. This form has been embraced in various languages, including Urdu, Hindi, Pashto, Turkish and Hebrew. Western poets such as Johann Wolfgang von Goethe and Federico García Lorca have experimented with the form.

A ghazal is composed of 5 to 15 couplets, each autonomous in structure and theme. Lines within the couplets are of uniform length. While traditional ghazals adhere to a strict meter, adaptations in English often offer more flexibility. The structure begins with a rhyme followed by a refrain in the first couplet, establishing a pattern that is echoed in the second line of subsequent couplets. Typically, the final couplet includes the poet's signature, referencing the author either directly or indirectly, and it often incorporates the poet's name or a play on it.

To inspire you, here is 'Yasmin' by British poet James Elroy Flecker (1884–1915), an English ghazal which observes the traditional restrictions of the form[4] (Flecker, 1916, pp 158–9):

'Yasmin'

How splendid in the morning glows the lily: with what grace he throws
His supplication to the rose: do roses nod **the head, Yasmin?**

But when the silver dove descends I find the little flower of friends
Whose very name that sweetly ends I say when I **have said, Yasmin.**

The morning light is clear and cold: I dare not in that light behold
A whiter light, a deeper gold, a glory too far shed, **Yasmin.**

But when the deep red eye of day is level with the lone highway,
And some to Meccah turn to pray, and I toward **thy bed, Yasmin;**

Or when the wind beneath the moon is drifting like a soul aswoon,
And harping planets talk love's tune with milky wings outspread, Yasmin,

Shower down thy love, O burning bright! For one night or the other night Will come **the Gardener** *in white, and gathered flowers* **are dead, Yasmin.**

Exercise: crafting a ghazal

This exercise involves creating a ghazal, a poetic form rich in emotional and philosophical depth, using an opening line from a renowned poet.

Choose one of the options offered below to use as the opening couplet of your ghazal:

1. The Truth must dazzle gradually
Or every man be blind (Emily Dickinson, nd)

2. Better by far you should forget and smile
Than that you should remember and be sad (Christina Rossetti, nd)

3. To see a World in a Grain of Sand
And a Heaven in a Wild Flower (William Blake, nd)

4. On your hearts imprint this lesson, Wisdom rife,
Love and Labour are the mainsprings
of all life (Emma Scarr Booth, 1893, p 157)

Write your ghazal:

- **Structure:** Compose a ghazal that includes 5 to 15 couplets. Each couplet should stand alone in terms of theme and structure yet tie together with the rest through a unified rhyme and refrain pattern.

- **Consistency:** Ensure each line within your couplets is of the same length. While traditional ghazals have a strict meter, you may choose to relax this in an English-language version.

- **Rhyme and refrain:** Start with a rhyme followed by a refrain in your first couplet. This sets up a scheme that should be mirrored in the second line of each subsequent couplet.

- **Concluding signature:** Typically, the final couplet of a ghazal includes a personal touch from the poet, often involving a mention of the poet's own name or a related term, giving a signature to the piece.

This exercise may seem daunting, particularly at this stage of the process, for some of you. You may like to refer to the section on figures of speech and techniques such as rhythm, rhyme and repetition. Once you go through that, you could come back and try working on a ghazal. However, others may want to engage now with the traditional structure of the ghazal. Infuse it with your personal creative touch, using the inspirational start provided by a famed poet.

Shape poems

In the Preface, we detailed the journey of developing this book, which included conducting workshops for both newcomers and experienced researchers interested in poetic inquiry. Among the various poetic forms introduced, shape poems were particularly well-received, being both accessible and impactful. We recommend this form as an excellent starting point.

A shape poem, or concrete poem, is designed to create a visual image with words on the page, akin to a calligram. This style blends literary and visual arts, engaging readers through the poem's text, layout, typography and visual portrayal of the theme. The structure of a shape poem is integral to its meaning, enhancing the expressive power of the words used.

The tradition of forming poems to represent ideas or images stretches back to ancient Africa and Greece. The 20th century saw a significant evolution of this form, with notable contributions from American poet e.e. cummings, French poet Guillaume Apollinaire and artistic movements like Surrealism in Latin America and Dadaism in Switzerland. These creators pioneered pattern poems that used word spacing and styling to achieve dramatic effects.

For researchers looking to incorporate shape poems into their projects, we recommend the following approach:

1. **Inspiration:** Explore existing shape poems to understand how others have leveraged this format. This can also help clarify your thematic focus.
2. **Theme selection:** Define the subject of your poem, which will guide the choice of an appropriate shape.

3. **Shape choice:** Brainstorm potential shapes that resonate with your theme. Opt for simple, recognisable forms that are easy to depict with text, such as a fruit or a bell.
4. **Sketch your poem:** Draw the chosen shape on paper to serve as a blueprint. You might experiment with placing words within this outline to see how they fit.
5. **Compose your poem:** With the structure outlined, start filling it in with text. Keep the words concise to maintain the integrity of the shape. Integrating terms that relate to the physical form of the poem can streamline this process.
6. **Text implementation:** Craft a narrative within the shape or use a selection of letters and words that repeat to complete the image. The poem can be in free verse; rhyming is optional.

Well-known early examples of shape poems are 'La verre' ('The glass') and 'La bouteille' ('The bottle') by 18th-century French poet Charles-François Panard (1689–1765)[5] (see Figure 2.2).

Tanya Layne, affiliated with an organisation dedicated to improving water governance, created the poem *Can We Be*

Figure 2.2: 'La verre' and 'La bouteille' by Charles-François Panard

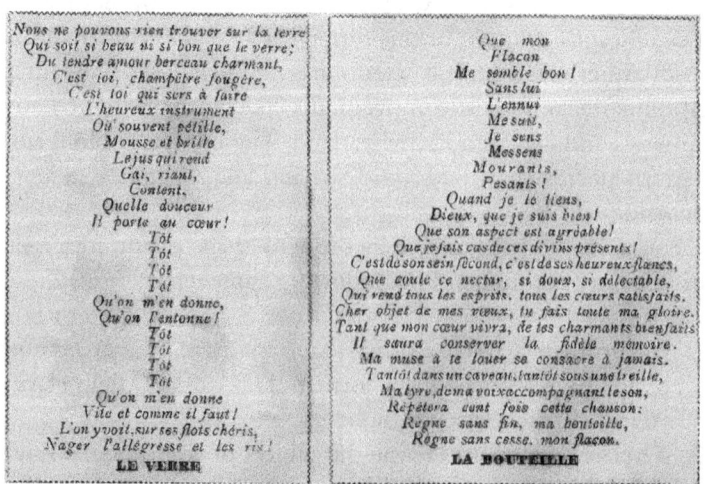

Source: Published in *Mon Dimanche* magazine 1906

The way of poems

Like Water? during one of our poetic inquiry workshops. This found poem distils insights from action research on social learning within water governance, developed through a public sector project with government and civil society partners. The poem's layout reflects its theme, symbolising both the appearance and the flexibility of water, contrasting sharply with rigid structures typical in hierarchical systems. Although not officially included in the project's documentation, this innovative poem effectively sparked discussions on methodology among diverse workshop participants.

'Can we be like water'

Innovation roadmap?

Towards

Water security

Others aren't listening

Usual predictable and boring

Challenging to understand each other

Different realities, different knowledge systems

Working emergently, with key principles, qualities inside

Cocreate, enable rather than cause, work with, not on or for

Connecting with intention, working emergently with what comes up

Deeply relational: openness, courage, presence, attentiveness to each moment

Authenticity and vulnerability receptive to discomfort accompanying new learning

Growing connection with ourselves, with others, with nature, with water, with flow

See and listen differently, participants in conflict can move, change their part, we can too

Relationships deepening, partnerships maturing, networks expanding, situations changing

We look at our self, our activities, our practice, how we are as we do what we do, our way of being

Deeply relational: caring, delicate expression extends across differences, challenging old imbalances

Paying attention to context, to movement, to relationship; without judgement, analysis, evaluation

See the essence, the essence guides us, we see our part, grow our practice, grow how we grow

Deeper understanding of the situation, deeper understanding of ourselves in the situation

Towards water security, a relational approach complements technical competencies

Bring both that they might best serve, invitation to begin engaging and learning

Learning and growing together in living catchments

Towards water security, innovation roadmap?

Towards water security

Pantoum

The pantoum is a poetic form that is particularly accessible to beginners and highly effective in workshops. Similar to a villanelle, it features repeating lines throughout the poem: it has four-line stanzas in which the second and fourth lines of each stanza serve as the first and third lines of the next stanza. This repetitive pattern significantly bolsters the poem's rhythm and emotional depth. Yvonne Sliep, one of the contributors to this book, wrote a pantoum to articulate her observations of a social justice project in the Democratic Republic of Congo, Africa.

'Kiliba Village, East DRC'

I remember the woman with the pointing finger
arm straight jabbing holes in the air
a village raped by soldiers, then raped by 'peace keepers'
the remaining men left – now it is a village of
only women

arm straight jabbing holes in the air
she carried her rags with a straight back
the remaining men left – now it is a village of
only women
her head draped in faded cloth, a head held high

she carried her rags with a straight back
with blazing eyes she told us in a loud voice
her head draped in faded cloth, a head held high
you do not tell us what we experienced or feel

with blazing eyes she told us in a loud voice
they have not broken our spirits and we will not lie down
you do not tell us what we experienced or feel
we stand up side by side to build our village and
our young

they have not broken our spirits and we will not lie down
a village raped by soldiers, then raped by 'peace keepers'

we stand up side by side to build our village and our young
I remember the woman with the pointing finger

Exercise: crafting a pantoum

Yvonne's poem is longer than a 12-line pantoum. But if you look at the first three stanzas of her poem, she employs the rules of the pantoum structure (see below) to good effect. The pantoum uses a specific repeating pattern that creates a looping effect, enhancing both the rhythmic and thematic continuity of the poem. Each couplet introduces new content while also connecting back to previous lines, creating a tightly integrated poetic form.

Here is how to structure a 12-line pantoum:

Line 1

Line 2

Line 3

Line 4

Line 5 (repeats Line 2)

Line 6

Line 7 (repeats Line 4)

Line 8

Line 9 (repeats line 6)

Line 10

Line 11 (repeat line 8)

> Line 12
> It is now your turn to have a go at creating a 12-line pantoum in response to a chosen stimulus, prompt or image.

The pantoum is the sixth and final poetic form we have introduced in this chapter. We now turn to figures of speech.

Figures of speech

Writers often turn to poetry to create a more vivid reality and to engage the reader's 'senses and sensibilities'. Figures of speech, alongside tools and techniques like repetition and rhythm (see Figure 2.3), are how this 'magic' is performed.[6]

A figure of speech, also known as rhetorical figure or figurative language, is a way of expressing ideas that strays from conventional word usage to convey deeper significance or emphasise a viewpoint. In literature, these are termed literary devices, while in rhetoric they are known as rhetorical devices. Figures of speech fall into two main categories: tropes and schemes. Tropes alter the literal meaning of words to express something figuratively, employing techniques like simile and apostrophe. Schemes, on the other hand, manipulate sound and syntax through methods such as alliteration and assonance, enhancing style and auditory effect.

The English language features numerous figures of speech that enrich both writing and everyday conversation. While it would be impractical to discuss all of them in detail here, recognising and understanding a few key examples is crucial for any poet, especially those involved in the scholarly creation of research poetry. We will concentrate on four primary figures of speech:

- simile;
- metaphor;
- personification;
- imagery.

Figure 2.3: Figures of speech

To demonstrate these, we will use Kirsten Deane's poem 'Fathers and sons' as an example.

Simile

A simile is a figure of speech that compares two fundamentally different objects or concepts by using the words 'like' or 'as'. These words act as connectors, establishing a basis for comparison. For example, saying someone moves 'as slow as a sloth' clearly illustrates their sluggish pace by comparing it to that of a notoriously slow-moving animal. To use similes effectively, the comparison should be to something familiar to the reader, helping them to grasp the characteristics being highlighted. This technique typically enhances the understanding or impact of a description by contrasting it with its opposite. Consider this stanza from Deane's poem:

> They're like nothing else
> not like dogs but lions
> who hunt in the same hunting ground

Deane aims to emphasise the extreme behaviour of the subject by comparing it to a lion rather than a dog. By contrasting two distinct species with different behaviours in a single line, she creates a divided image. This contrast helps the reader visualise the differences between the two animals. The effectiveness of the poem stems from encouraging readers to engage in visualisation, requiring their attention and interaction with the poem.

> ### Exercise: enhancing your poem with similes
>
> 1. **Add similes:** Continue the poem you started in the narrative poems section. Incorporate three to four similes to describe the characters in your poem.
>
> 2. **Choose relatable comparisons:** Use similes that compare your characters to things most readers would recognise or have experience with.
>
> 3. **Reflect on impact:** Write four to five points about how these similes affect your poem and its characters, considering their contribution to the readers' understanding and engagement.

Metaphor

Metaphors, like similes, are a powerful way to draw comparisons and enhance the reader's understanding of the subject's characteristics. However, unlike similes, metaphors present a direct equivalence without allowing room for doubt; they assert that one thing is another, omitting comparative words such as 'like' and 'as'. This absence makes the comparison implicit, offering no invitation to question why the comparison is made. Essentially, a metaphor fuses two disparate elements into a cohesive description.

For example, the expression 'tears were a river flowing down her cheeks' is a metaphor because: (a) it directly equates tears with a river without the use of 'like' or 'as'; and (b) it contrasts the small, line-like tears with the expansive body of a river, highlighting their conceptual opposition. By describing the tears as a river, the metaphor vividly conveys the depth of the subject's emotions, allowing the reader to feel their profound sadness or joy. An example of a metaphor can be found in the second stanza of Deane's poem:

> *They hunch down*
> *they are boneless babies*
> *and they eye the springbok.*

In these lines, the subjects (the fathers and the sons) are metaphorically described as 'boneless babies'. This imagery shows that a metaphor can offer a richer description than a simple comparison. Since the metaphor does not invite the reader to question the likeness between the subjects and what they are compared to, it immerses the reader directly into the scene being depicted.

Exercise: enhancing your poem with metaphors

To practice using metaphors, you could return to the narrative poem where you have been developing a character. Enhance your portrayal by incorporating three metaphors that offer deeper insights into your character's behaviour. Consider using animals, natural elements or other familiar objects as metaphors to vividly convey aspects of the character.

Exercise: reflecting on being lost and finding your way

This exercise starts with reading the following poem *Lost* by David Wagoner:

> *Stand still. The trees ahead and bushes beside you*
> *Are not lost. Wherever you are is called Here,*

And you must treat it as a powerful stranger,

Must ask permission to know it and be known.
The forest breathes. Listen. It answers,
I have made this place around you.
If you leave it, you may come back again, saying Here.
No two trees are the same to Raven.
No two branches are the same to Wren.
If what a tree or a bush does is lost on you,
You are surely lost. Stand still. The forest knows
Where you are. You must let it find you.

1. **Initial reflection:** Once you have read the poem, think about a time when you felt lost, whether physically, morally, or emotionally. Record the details of that environment: list what you saw, heard and smelled, and concentrate on your physical sensations during this moment.

2. **Writing exercise:** Write to reconcile with that moment. Embed the environmental details into your body's memory, examining how these sensory experiences might merge with your physical feelings.

3. **Creating a poetic roadmap:** Recall a time when you felt lost in a non-geographical way, such as feeling emotionally or morally uncertain. Write a poem that maps the way back to a state of comfort. This can include the actual steps you took or ones you wish you had taken. Your goal is to guide yourself back to a place of inner peace and self-awareness, creating a dual map – one literal, one metaphorical – back to your core self.

This second exercise not only allows you to work with metaphors but also promotes deep reflection and creative expression. It helps you process feelings of being lost and guides you in charting a path back to familiarity and understanding.

Personification

Personification is a literary device where non-human, or inanimate objects are given human traits or qualities. For example, saying 'the wind whispered through the night' attributes the human action of whispering to the wind. This technique can be seen as a way to bring objects to life. For instance, describing a blanket as if it 'let out a heavy sigh' turns it into something that appears to live and breathe, giving it human-like qualities. We now turn to another poem by Kirsten Deane, 'Little pains', which effectively uses personification to enhance its themes.

'Little Pains'

It's quite pathetic, really.
The fact that I'm in pain for the most part. But still,
I only concentrate on the little pains –
my nail broke in half tonight.

I decided to paint onto my fingerskin.
It burnt, of course
but well worth it. The burn
was pretty harsh
and ladylike. My other pain
is dressed as a boy,
stubborn
and angry.

Other days, like today, it is my bowel movements that grab my attention.
I haven't shat in three days. This makes my mother worry
and I'm sure my skin
is tearing from the inside. My pain has found its way all around my body.

The little pains
I take them on dates
they're very polite,
I take them on seconds.

In the final stanza ('The little pains/I take them on dates/they're very polite,/I take them on seconds'), the poem personifies pains by describing them as 'polite', a trait typically associated only with human behaviour.

> ### Exercise: integrating personification into your poem
>
> 1. **Add personification:** Enhance the poem you are developing by including three instances of personification.
>
> 2. **Humanise an object**: Choose an object to feature in your poem and give it human characteristics that relate to your character.
>
> 3. **Illustrate relationships:** Use the personified object to reveal and enhance the relationship between the object and your main character(s), helping the reader understand their connection more deeply.

Imagery

Imagery in poetry involves using vivid and descriptive language to enhance the reader's experience by appealing to their senses. This technique involves the five senses – sight, sound, taste, touch and smell – which are essential for interacting with the world. By weaving these sensory details into poetry, they help advance the narrative and bring the poem to life, serving as key tools for description and often as the poem's foundation. Examples include 'I saw a peacock train rattling' for sight, 'the child screamed when the bee stung him' for sound, 'the habanero set my tongue on fire' for taste, 'her skin is pure silk' for touch and 'the familiar aroma of fresh-cut meadows in the air' for smell.

In 'Little pains', Deane uses imagery effectively: 'The burn/ was pretty harsh/and ladylike', using the sense of touch to convey pain vividly. When emotions are described in such a visceral, sensory manner, it allows the reader to empathise deeply with the poet's experience.

In this section, we have delved into figures of speech like similes, metaphors, personification and imagery, which enrich poetry by making it more vivid and engaging. These tools enhance the aesthetic quality of a poem and deepen the reader's understanding and emotional engagement.

Using these techniques thoughtfully affects a poem's tone, rhythm and overall impact. They are crucial for poets looking to transform their writing into a compelling art form. Through examples and exercises, we have shown how mastering these devices can greatly enhance your poetry's expressive power, enabling you to convey complex emotions and ideas effectively.

The three 'r's: repetition, rhythm and rhyme in poetry

The three foundational techniques in poetry – **repetition, rhythm** and **rhyme** – significantly enhance a poem's musicality, structure and emotional impact. If you are new to poetry, mastering these techniques may not come easily. However, like any skill, they can be developed over time with practice and application. As you become more adept at using these techniques, your poetic inquiries will become richer and more nuanced. So, continue to engage with the upcoming sections, even when doubts arise or you feel discouraged. Table 2.2 provides a definition and the purpose for each of these critical poetic elements.

Repetition, rhythm and rhyme are essential tools in poetry, each serving several important functions. They enhance the beauty and musicality of poetry, making it more pleasurable to read and listen to; they simplify the memorisation and recall of poems; they intensify the emotional impact of a poem by emphasising its themes, which deepens audience engagement with the content; and they provide structure, helping poets to organise their thoughts and convey them with artistic clarity.

At the beginning of this section, we categorised figures of speech into two main groups: tropes and schemes. Tropes transform the literal meaning of words to convey a figurative sense, using techniques like simile and epistrophe. Schemes, on the other hand, manipulate sound and syntax through various forms of repetition to enhance the auditory quality of poetry.

Table 2.2: Repetition, rhythm and rhyme

	Definition	Purpose
Repetition	Repetition involves deliberately using the same words, phrases, lines or structures multiple times within a poem.	It emphasises key themes or ideas, reinforces messages and enhances the overall musical flow of a poem. Repetition can also create a sense of unity and cohesion, making the poem more memorable and impactful.
Rhythm	Rhythm refers to the pattern of stressed and unstressed syllables in lines of poetry. It is what gives poetry its musical cadence and flow.	Rhythm helps to set the pace and mood of a poem, influencing how it is read and perceived. It can convey emotions effectively, build suspense or create a soothing effect, depending on the pattern used.
Rhyme	Rhyme is the repetition of similar sounding words, occurring at the end of lines in poems or songs.	Rhyme adds to the musicality of a poem, making it more pleasing and engaging to read or hear. It can also strengthen the structure of a poem, linking ideas and contributing to its aesthetic appeal.

Repetition

Repetition is a key technique used by poets to underline important themes, foster a sense of cohesion throughout the poem and elicit emotional responses from the reader. Here are some common figures of speech that involve repetition:

- **Anaphora:** the repetition of a word or phrase at the beginning of successive clauses or lines, which can build momentum and create a powerful emotional effect;
- **Epistrophe:** the repetition of a word or phrase at the end of successive clauses or lines, often used to emphasise a concept or idea;
- **Alliteration:** the repetition of initial consonant sounds in words close to each other, which can enhance the musical quality of a poem;
- **Assonance:** the repetition of vowel sounds within words close to each other to create internal rhyming within phrases or sentences, adding to the poem's auditory appeal.

Rhythm

Rhythm in poetry is the pattern of stressed and unstressed syllables in lines of verse. It is what makes poetry sound like music when read aloud. Rhythm creates a flow that can affect the pace and mood of the poem, contributing to its overall musicality. Key aspects include:

- **Meter:** a recurring pattern of stressed (strong) and unstressed (weak) syllabic beats in a line of poetry – common metrical patterns include iambic pentameter, trochaic tetrameter, and dactylic, each creating different rhythmic effects;
- **Cadence:** the modulation or inflection of the voice when reading the poem aloud – this gives the poem its rhythmic rise and fall, helping to convey emotions and emphasise particular words or phrases.

Rhyme

Rhyme is one of the easiest to recognise rhetorical devices and appears in songs and in many poetic forms, including, among others, limericks, sonnets, villanelles, etc. Here are some examples.

- **End rhyme:** This is a rhyme that occurs in the last syllables of the verse, like in the following limerick:

    There once was a farmer from **Leeds (A)**
    Who swallowed a packet of **seeds. (A)**
    It soon came to **pass, (B)**
    He was covered with **grass, (B)**
    But has all the tomatoes he **needs. (A)**

- **Internal rhyme:** This is a rhyme that occurs inside the line(s). A single line can contain internal rhyme (with multiple words in the same line rhyming), or the rhyming words can occur across multiple lines. Here is an example of internal rhyme from the opening stanza of 'The cloud' by Romantic poet Percy Bysshe Shelley:

    I bring fresh **showers** for the thirsting **flowers**,
    From the seas and the streams;
    I bear light **shade** for the leaves when **laid**

In their noonday dreams.
From my wings are **shaken** the dews that **waken**
The sweet buds every one,
When rocked to **rest** on their mother's **breast**,
As she dances about the sun.
I wield the **flail** of the lashing **hail**,
And whiten the green plains under,
And then **again** I dissolve it in **rain**,
And laugh as I pass in thunder.

- **Half rhyme or imperfect rhyme, sometimes called near-rhyme, lazy rhyme or slant rhyme:** This is when assonance and consonance are used to connect words that technically do not rhyme but have similar sounds. Here is an example from the poem 'Easter 1916' by William Butler Yeats:

    I have met them at close of day
    Coming with vivid **faces**
    From counter or desk among grey
    Eighteenth-century **houses**.

Exercise: developing rhythm, rhyme and repetition

This exercise is designed to help beginners in poetry to practice and enhance their understanding of rhythm, rhyme and repetition. We give you three ways in which you can explore each of these tools. You may need to do additional work to get to fully understand the different meters or rhyme schemes. Give it a try. For many, us included, it is often easier to start with repetition. If that is the case for you, then try that exercise instead.

Step 1: Rhythm practice

1. **Understanding meter:** Begin by reading a selection of poems that showcase different rhythmic patterns.

Identify the meter used in each (that is, iambic pentameter, trochaic tetrameter, and so on).

2. **Create your rhythmic line:** Write a four-line stanza choosing one type of meter. Focus on maintaining the same rhythmic pattern in each line to create a steady flow.

Step 2: Rhyme development

1. **Rhyme scheme identification:** Select a poem and identify its rhyme scheme (for example, ABAB, AABB, ABBA). Analyse how the rhyme affects the poem's structure and mood.
2. **Craft a rhyming stanza:** Write a four-line stanza using one of the rhyme schemes you have studied. Try to make the rhymes natural without forcing your word choices.

Step 3: Repetition techniques

1. **Identify repetition:** Choose a poem that effectively uses repetition and note how it enhances the poem's theme or emotional weight.
2. **Implement repetition:** Write a poem or a stanza that includes:
   - anaphora (repetition at the start of lines): repeat the same word or phrase at the beginning of at least three consecutive lines;
   - epistrophe (repetition at the end of lines): repeat the same word or phrase at the end of at least three consecutive lines.

Figures of speech are essential tools for writers to enhance vividness, introduce new ideas and build compelling arguments.

However, their use should be measured. When used sparingly and thoughtfully, figures of speech can greatly enrich your writing. Overuse, however, can overwhelm the reader and weaken the impact. It is often beneficial to maintain a consistent metaphor throughout a poem. In both poetic inquiry and broader poetry, the principle of 'less is more' is often applicable. Polish poet and Nobel Prize laureate Wisława Szymborska (nd) captures this sentiment well: 'The fear of straight speaking, the constant, painstaking efforts to metaphorise everything, the ceaseless need to prove you're a poet in every line: these are the anxieties that beset every budding bard. But they are curable, if caught in time.'

Conclusion

In this chapter, we have explored the fundamental aspect of poetic inquiry: poetry itself. As tsitsistas (Cheyenne) poet Lance Henson puts it: 'Poems are stories that reflect the human experience, expressing the relationship between a person and the forces impacting their life' (Henson, 2009, p 7). This perspective prompts an essential question for poet-researchers: how can we narrate our stories in ways that are truthful, thoughtful, rigorous and creative? This chapter has introduced and exemplified key figures of speech such as metaphor, simile, personification and imagery. It has also highlighted the importance of rhythm, rhyme and repetition, urging readers to use these elements thoughtfully in their poetic endeavours. Moreover, the chapter has reviewed popular poetic forms and shown how they can convey strong, clear and impactful messages. Aimed at enhancing the poetic skills of both experienced and budding poets, this practice-oriented chapter broadens readers' understanding and application of poetry.

Notes

[1] It is contested whether Afrikaans came from Europe and that a version of it existed in South Africa with indigenous people before colonisation.
[2] This section draws extensively from Brewer (2014).
[3] This section draws from poets.org: https://poets.org/glossary/ghazal.
[4] A masterful example of traditional ghazal written in English is Patricia Smith's 'Hip Hop Ghazal', available at: https://www.poetryfoundation.org/poetrymagazine/poems/49642/hip-hop-ghazal

⁵ Two recent fascinating examples of shape poems are 'Needles' by Brian Bilston, which resembles a Christmas tree (https://brianbilston.com/2021/12/06/needles/), and 'Swan and Shadow' by John Hollander, which beautifully recreates the profile of a swan and its reflection on the water (www.poetryfoundation.org/poetrymagazine/browse?volume=109&issue=3&page=35).

⁶ This section re-elaborates and summarises information on this topic available in various websites, including masterclass.com, literarydevices.net and Merriem-Webster, 'Useful rhetorical devices': www.merriam-webster.com/grammar/rhetorical-devices-list-examples

References

Almudéver Chanzà, J. (2021) *(Re)inventions and (Dis)continuations of the Catholic Tradition: Community-Making in a Spanish Village*, PhD thesis, University of Edinburgh.

Angelou, M. (nd) 'Kin', available at: www.poetryfoundation.org/poems/48987/kin-56d22aaaea246

Bintz, William P. (2023) Writing golden shovel poetry across the curriculum, *Texas Journal of Literacy Education*, 10(1): 25–45.

Blake, W. (nd) 'Auguries of innocence', available at: www.poetryfoundation.org/poems/43650/auguries-of-innocence

Booth, E.S. (1893) *The Family of Three, Iesuina and Other Poems*, Buffalo: Charles Welles Moulton.

Brewer, R.L. (2020) *The Complete Guide of Poetic Forms: 100+ Poetic Form Definitions and Examples for Poets*, Writer's Digest.

Brooks, G. (nd) 'We real cool', available at: www.poetryfoundation.org/poetrymagazine/poems/28112/we-real-cool

Brown, D. (1998) *Voicing the Text: South African Oral Poetry and Performance*, Cape Town: Oxford University Press.

Brown, D. (2006) *To Speak of This Land: Identity and Belonging in South Africa and Beyond*, Pietermaritzburg: University of KwaZulu-Natal Press.

Brown, J. (2020) 'Stay', in *The Tradition*, Port Townsend: Copper Canyon Press, p 108.

Chambers, L. et al (2024) '"We will not be silenced": using poetic performance to mobilise the stories of African/African-descendant women living with HIV who work in Canadian HIV service work', in H. van Rooyen and K. Pithouse-Morgan (eds) *Poetic Inquiry for the Human and Social Sciences: Voices from the South and North*, Cape Town: HSRC Press, pp 33–50.

Chao G. (1997) 'Mongolian oral epic poetry: an overview', *Oral Tradition*, 12(2): 322–36.

Clunies, R.M. (1986) 'Australian Aboriginal oral traditions', *Oral Tradition* 1(2): 231–71.

d'Abdon, R. (2013) 'Migrant blues', in *Sunnyside Nightwalk*, Johannesburg: Geko, p 23.

Dhlomo, H.I.E. (1977) 'Zulu folk poetry', *English in Africa*, 4(2): 43–59.

Dickinson, E. (nd) 'Tell all the truth but tell it slant', available at: www.poetryfoundation.org/poems/56824/tell-all-the-truth-but-tell-it-slant-1263

Eliot, S.L.P. (1937) *Stories from The Thousand and One Nights* (trans E. William Lane), New York: Collins and Son.

Finnegan, R. (1970) *Oral Literature in Africa*, Oxford: The Clarendon Press.

Flecker, J.E. (1916) *The Collected Poems of James Elroy Flecker*, New York: Doubleday.

Garuba, H. (2003) 'Poetry and poetics', in S. Gikandi (ed) *Encyclopaedia of African Literature*, London: Routledge, pp 609–10.

Gross, L.W. (2016) *Anishinaabe Ways of Knowing and Being*, London: Routledge.

Gunner, L. (ed) (1994) *Politics and Performance: Theatre Poetry and Song in Southern Africa*, Johannesburg: Wits University Press.

Hatto, A. (2017) *The World of the Khanty Epic Hero-princes: An Exploration of a Siberian Oral Tradition*, Cambridge: Cambridge University Press.

Hayes, T. (2010) *Lighthead*, New York: Penguin.

Henson, L. (2009) *The Missing Bead: Dog Soldier Poems Written in Exile*, Milano: Arcipelago.

Hofmeyer, I. (1993) *We Spend Our Years as a Tale That Is Told: Oral Historical Narrative in a South African Chiefdom*, Johannesburg: Wits University Press.

Hull, K. (2016) 'The Ch'orti' Maya myths of creation', *Oral Tradition*, 30(1): 3–26.

Kaschula, R.H. (ed) (1993) *Foundations in Southern African Oral Literature*, Johannesburg: Wits University Press.

Kaschula, R.H. (2002) *The Bones of the Ancestors Are Shaking: Xhosa Oral Poetry in Context*, Cape Town: Juta.

Keylock, M. (2014) 'No easy stroll to freedom for SA poetry's restless howler', *Mail & Guardian*, 15 August, available at: https://mg.co.za/article/2014-08-15-no-easy-stroll-to-freedom-for-sa-poetrys-restless-howler/

Kgositsile, K. (nd) 'A brief word on poetry', *African Writing Online*, available at: www.african-writing.com/eleven/kgositsile.htm

Klara, K. and Harris, F. (2019) *A Diné History of Navajoland*, Tucson: The University of Arizona Press.

Krog, A. (2004) *The Stars Say 'Tsau': /Xam Poetry of Dia!kwain, Kweiten-ta-//ken, /A!kunta, Han#kass'o, and //Kabbo*, Cape Town: Kwela Books.

Kunene, D.P. (1971) *Heroic Poetry of the Basotho*, Oxford: Clarendon Press.

Kunene, M. (1961) *An Analytical Survey of Zulu Poetry both Traditional and Modern*, Unpublished master's thesis, University of Natal, Durban, South Africa.

Lutz, Hartmut. (2002) *Approaches: Essays in Native North American Studies and Literatures*, Vol. 11, [Augsburg, Germany]: Wissner, p 199.

Mahungana, S.J. (1999) 'The relevance of Xitsonga oral tradition', *Alternation*, 6(1): 37–54.

Maimane, K.C. and Mathonsi, N. (2021) 'Echoes of lithoko in modern Sesotho poetry: an intertextual perspective', *Literator*, 42(1): art a1657. doi: 10.4102/lit.v42i1.1657

McRae, J. (2017) *Maori Oral Tradition: He Korero no te Ao Tawhito*, Auckland: Auckland University Press.

Okpewho, I. (ed) (1990) *The Oral Performance in Africa*, Ibadan: Spectrum Books.

Opland, J. (1983) *Xhosa Oral Poetry: Aspects of a South African Tradition*, Johannesburg: Ravan Press.

Opland, J. (1998) *Xhosa Poets and Poetry*, Cape Town: David Philip Publishers.

Otono, N. (2021) 'Orality, masculinity and narrative strategies in The Arabian Nights', in N. Otiono and C. Akoma (eds) *Oral Literary Performance in Africa: Beyond Text*, New York: Routledge, pp 81–95.

Phakathi, V. (2021) 'The trinity of poetry – what is poetry? An introduction by Vus'umuzi Phakathi', available at: www.poetrypotion.com/the-trinity-of-poetry-what-is-poetry%E2%80%8B-an-introduction-by-vusumuzi-phakathi/

Phalafala, U. (2024) *Keorapetse Kgositsile & The Black Arts Movement*, Johannesburg: Wits University Press.
Rossetti, C. (nd) 'Remember', available at: www.poetryfoundation.org/poems/45000/remember-56d224509b7ae
Sequeira, J. (2023) 'Mapuche poetry as global intellectual history', *Global Intellectual History*, 8: 229–40.
Shelley, P.B. (nd) 'The cloud', available at: www.poetryfoundation.org/poems/45117/the-cloud-56d2247bf4112
Sone, E.M. (2011) 'Swazi oral literature studies yesterday and today: the way forward', *The Southern African Journal for Folklore Studies*, 21: 39–53.
Szymborska, W. (nd) 'How to (and how not to) write poetry', available at: www.poetryfoundation.org/articles/68657/how-to-and-how-not-to-write-poetry-56d2484397277
van Rooyen, H. and d'Abdon, R. (2020) 'Transforming data into poems: poetic inquiry practices for social and human sciences', *Education As Change*, 24, available at: https://unisapressjournals.co.za/index.php/EAC/article/view/8103/4803
Vilakazi, B.W. (1945) *The Oral and Written Literature in Nguni*, Unpublished PhD thesis, University of the Witwatersrand, Johannesburg, South Africa.
Vilakazi, B.W. (1993) 'The conception and development of poetry in Zulu', in R.H. Kaschula (ed) *Foundations in Southern African Oral Literature*, Johannesburg: Wits University Press, pp 55–84.
Walker, B.N.O. (nd) 'A mojave lullaby', available at: https://poets.org/poem/mojave-lullaby
Webber, S. (2008) 'Arab and Berber oral traditions in North Africa', in F.A. Irele and S. Gikandi (eds) *Cambridge History of African and Caribbean Literature*, Cambridge: Cambridge University Press, pp 49–70.
White, L. (2003) 'Basque Bertsolaritza', *Oral Tradition*, 18(1): 142–3.
Zedda, P. (2009) 'The southern Sardinian tradition of the Mutetu Longu: a functional analysis', *Oral Tradition*, 24(1): 3–40.

3

Taking poetry into research

Angela Hough, Yvonne Sliep and Heidi van Rooyen

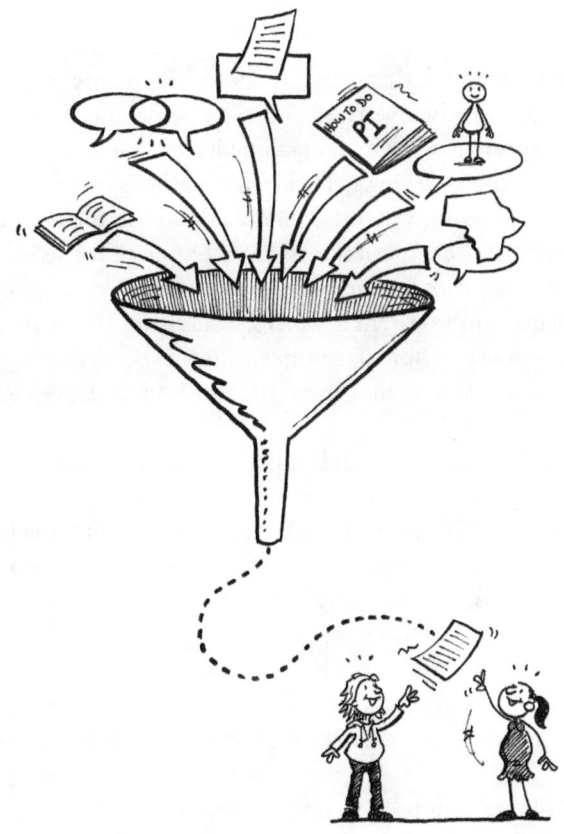

> In this chapter, we explore the concept of poetic inquiry in more detail. We outline four aspects: (1) a decolonial approach to poetic inquiry; (2) the role of poetry in enriching research; (3) found and generated poems; and (4) guidelines for creating research poems. While we emphasise that poetic inquiry can be used at various stages from researcher reflection to exploration of texts and literature to dissemination of research findings, we focus on practical guidance for crafting poems using data within research contexts. Our aim is to spark your curiosity and encourage you to tailor these approaches to your own research needs.

Introduction

Research aims to uncover truths about life, nature and human experiences. Qualitative research, in particular, delves deep into human experiences such as attachment, loss and sexuality using storytelling and interviews. Traditional methods often summarise these interviews into themes, potentially losing the essence and complexity of the experiences shared. Different forms of poetic expression can capture the uniqueness and diversity of research participants' and researchers' voices, addressing concerns that in qualitative research voices have been appropriated, overpowered, over-summarised or even silenced (Richardson, 2002; van Rooyen and d'Abdon, 2020).

Poetry, with its vivid and distilled language, can translate these experiences into a more potent form, capturing their essence and paradoxes in fewer words. Recognising that all knowledge is influenced by the perspectives of the researcher, poetry offers a narrative approach to making sense of our worlds and identities (Butler-Kisber, 2002).

This chapter builds on what you have learnt about the craft of poetry and looks at how you can use poetry and poems as a methodology in your research. We focus on the following aspects:

- a decolonial approach to poetic inquiry;
- the role of poetry in enriching research;

- an introduction to various types of poetic inquiry;
- guidelines for creating research poems.

There is a wealth of exciting material to explore, so let us get started.

A decolonial and poetic inquiry lens

Building on the discussions in Chapter 1, we delve deeper into how colonisation has not only systematically silenced diverse voices but also established the colonisers' scientific methods and knowledge as the dominant norm. These practices often overshadow and undervalue alternative ways of being and knowing. Poetic inquiry emerges as a potent tool for decolonisation, challenging these long-standing norms and offering a new perspective on understanding and valuing knowledge.

To anchor our discussion, we draw inspiration from the Peace Prayer of Saint Francis, as compiled by Reverend Hiram Brett from the Connecticut Mental Health Center and adapted it to reflect the ethos of poetic inquiry in a decolonial context.

'Manifesto of poetic inquiry'

Poetic inquiry, make me your instrument:
Where there is 'assumed objectivity' let me recognise my position
Where there is abstraction, let me give context and detail
Where there is entitlement, let me recognise intersections of privilege.
Where there is extraction of knowledge, let me acknowledge where ideas come from.

Poetic inquiry grant that I may
Not so much seek to be heard
as to hear those voices that have been silenced
and marginalised:
To hear the queer voices, the voices of women and those differently abled;
To know that black lives matter.

Poetic inquiry grant that I may be reflexive in my inquiry
Intersectional in my awareness
Participatory in my inclusion and inclusive in
my participation.
Grant that I may not so much seek
to be understood as to understand.

This adaptation sets the stage for an exploration of how poetic inquiry can subvert 'Euro-Western' academic narratives and validate diverse, often marginalised, ways of knowing. This approach not only challenges the conventional view of scientific research as neutral and objective but also highlights its often-extractive nature. Traditional research methods can strip away context and reduce lived experiences to mere data points, frequently positioning the researcher as the sole interpreter of knowledge.

In contrast, critical research approaches, such as poetic inquiry, foreground the voices of participants, allowing their experiences to resonate directly and powerfully. This method transforms discovered themes into various expressive formats that provoke deeper understanding beyond the capabilities of standard research methodologies.

Consider, for example, a poem that captures the conflicting identities of African priests who are gay, illustrating the profound fear that their faith and queerness cannot coexist without endangering their family ties or damaging the public perception of the church (Kaunda and Fubah, 2023). Poetic inquiry brings these complex, often suppressed narratives to light, offering insights into personal and social dilemmas that traditional research might overlook. Through such expressions, poetic inquiry not only informs but also enriches the academic discourse with nuanced perspectives.

'I am gay'

But I can't come out
Because I'm a priest
I'm an African
Only my inner circle of queer friends
Know my most guarded 'holy shit'
The reality of being pigeonholed

And being a queer priest is a real terror
That God is using me as the 'other' is the only hope
The only hope I cling to amidst tears and fears
From the periphery to the front row
Yet pigeonholed   I want to come out for my freedom
But I can't dare because I am a priest
I'm an African
I have a family name to protect
I have a church image to preserve
Can there be any good news from the pigeonholed clergy?

Decolonisation seeks to expose and dismantle the pervasive power structures built through colonialism that continue to shape our world. By challenging the Eurocentric and Western biases embedded in our language, thought processes, curricula and research methodologies, it advocates for a research paradigm that embraces diversity, promotes equality and cultivates self-awareness. This approach emphasises the importance of centring the experiences of marginalised groups. As writers, researchers and academics, we have a duty to address and reform the systemic inequalities in educational and research settings that uphold colonial and apartheid legacies (Sibiya and Ndaba, 2023).

Poetic inquiry aims to *acknowledge* knowledge lineages, to celebrate resilience, to recognise living systems, diversity and other ways of knowing. It recognises there is not one way or system of knowledge, but rather multiple voices, and that current knowledge builds on indigenous knowledge systems. This means being careful about how we engage people in research, making sure they give permission, that their voice is heard and acknowledged, that we reflect our learning back to participants, that we make the information accessible, that we keep listening and learning.

It aims to *not be extractive*. So even though we may use the words of participants, we aim to do this in ways that are respectful and collaborative and not 'othering'. It requires an openness to listening, to hearing, to knowing in different ways, to hearing silenced or marginalised voices, especially if one comes from a dominant culture or voice. It requires reflecting on difficulties and parts of relating that may get lost in translation.

Positionality acknowledges the social and political context that creates your identity in terms of race, class, gender, sexuality and ability status. It also describes how your identity influences, and potentially biases, your understanding of and outlook on the world.

Othering refers to the process where an individual or group of people attribute negative characteristics to other individuals or groups of people that set them apart as representing that which is opposite to or different from them.

Poetic inquiry recognises that all knowledge is inherently *positional* and *dependent* on the observer's biases and perspective.

This approach challenges the notion of neutrality often claimed in conventional research methods and emphasises reflexivity instead.

Researchers are encouraged to openly acknowledge their biases and contexts – the lenses through which they view research participants – and embrace a willingness to learn and adapt. The act of writing poetry is not just a creative output but a method of inquiry that can catalyse new understandings and insights, underscoring the dynamic and exploratory nature of poetic inquiry. This process highlights the importance of *self-awareness* and adaptability in research, fostering a deeper engagement with the subject matter and enriching the exploration process.

Malika Ndlovu (van Rooyen et al, 2023) reflects on research conducted by an English-speaking researcher with Xhosa-speaking people who have a profound connection to their ancestral land. The poem highlights how meaning can be lost – not only through translation but also due to differing conceptual understandings and power dynamics. Through this poem, the researcher-poet contemplates the disconnect, enabling a deeper form of listening. By presenting this potential gap, the poem invites readers to acknowledge and reflect on these nuances, rather than overlook their existence. The following is an extract from Ndlovu's poem 'Opening and anchoring'.

'Opening and anchoring'

The land and the language
The language of the land
The mother and her tongue
Motherland tones, lengthening shadows
Call for listening deeper than data
Difference between the choice to stay silent
And misunderstanding, assumptions of consent
Eroding faith in the process, echoing previous promises
The land and the language
The language of the land
Underground currents of emotion
Fleshing out the bones of English words
IsiXhosa voicing, lyricism and repetition
Unearthing more questions, in pursuit of wider truth
The capturer discovers her heart's ears can clarify
Realign intentions, ground authentic conversation.

Exercise: exploring decolonial poetic inquiry

We have discussed the role of poetic inquiry in challenging and deconstructing dominant knowledge systems and power dynamics within research. Let us take a moment to reflect on what we have learned and apply this understanding creatively.

Individual reflection:

- Choose one of the three poems discussed: the 'Manifesto of poetic inquiry', 'I am gay' or the section of Malika Ndlovu's 'Opening and anchoring'.

- Reflect on how each poem addresses decolonial themes. Identify the power dynamics discussed and consider how these poems challenge traditional research paradigms.

- Think about how the use of poetic inquiry in these texts influences your understanding of knowledge and power in research.

Creating the space for conversation, partnership and collaboration

A decolonial perspective values *relationship, partnership* and *connection*. In a world grappling with inequalities, pandemics such as COVID-19, wars and polarisation, poetry offers a means to embrace nuance and reconcile opposites in our human experiences. At a time when the potential for connection is diminishing, poetry allows us to see from another's perspective with compassion. Dalal (2014) proposes new ways of thinking that are relational and non-hierarchical, and which aspire to decoloniality, recognising that we are all part of an interconnected web, both trivial and profound. Often the academic researcher's voice can be seen as superior or having ownership of knowing and knowledge. Poetic inquiry can decolonise conventional knowledge production through co-creation and partnership with participants at all stages of the research process, from crafting the research question to the approach, analysis, writing and dissemination of the research (van Rooyen and Pithouse-Morgan, 2024).

'The Poet'

She is sensitive
Some say overly so
She feels deeply
Some say overly so
She hears the voices
That are unheard
She sees moments
That others rush over

She feels where
The world wants us numb
She dares to be different where
The world wants us uniformed
She speaks her unique truth where
The world defines normal

Her words resist
in quiet rebellion

A claiming of love and loss
A claiming of what is human
A delicate activism
She refuses to put down.

Poetry often facilitates a dialogue between the poet and the audience, the poet and their experiences and, in the case of poetic inquiry, the researcher and participants with specific experiences. This dialogue may also involve self-reflection. By fostering such conversations, we invite multiple perspectives, embrace uncertainty and 'stay with the trouble' of complex themes, which can reveal new insights to both ourselves and potentially a wider audience. This engagement involves our entire being – body, mind and heart – as we seek to understand each other or our own experiences. Our perspectives can be intra-psychic (within ourselves), inter-psychic (between people) or systemic.

Bayo Akomolafe (2018) promotes the concept of listening with 'thin ears', which focuses on observing without prematurely seeking solutions, attentively hearing the underlying nuances and giving space to voices that are often overshadowed by dominant narratives (this is illustrated in Figure 3.1). As explored in Chapter 2, poems can take various forms – narrative, conversational or confrontational – each offering unique ways to express viewpoints. Poetry aims to capture and convey the deeper truths of experiences or perspectives, remaining receptive

Figure 3.1: Listening with thin ears

DEEP LISTENING.   BENEATH THE SURFACE.

to insights that surface subtly and enrich our understanding beyond the obvious, often revealing what our conscious minds might overlook.

Collaborations between interviewers and those interviewed, particularly in research, are founded on trust and reciprocity. Such partnerships allow for intersecting stories and insights to surface, helping to balance power differentials. It is crucial to build trust and respect, and to practice researcher reflexivity (Butler-Kisber, 2002). As van Rooyen and d'Abdon (2020, 2023) have shown, co-constructing poems with participants is also an important aspect of this process.

Creativity involves effort and grappling with our subject matter. We bring our personal perspectives, observations and essence to this process. As we delve deeper, meaning unfolds naturally and the poem takes shape. Our pursuit of creativity is essential to life, a sentiment echoed by musician Nick Cave in a letter read by Stephen Fry in his discussion on the nature of creativity (Letters Live, 2023).

Lynn Norton (Sliep et al, 2024) reflects on the collaborative aspect of research and the collective journey of poetic inquiry in the following extract:

> *we lived through different stories*
> *tearing information into pieces*
> *sewing back a tapestry of poetry*
> *new connections shaping me*
> *searching for essence*
> *a new truth moulded*
> *new life sprouting*
> *together we built*
>
> *we co-create a map*
> *that will be tested for accuracy*
> *reflecting*
> *framing*
> *checking*
> *charting*
> *an in between the spaces*
> *writing poetry that speaks loudly*

> ### Exercise: writing your decolonial manifesto
>
> To conclude this section, we invite you to engage in a creative exercise that draws on your personal and cultural perspectives:
>
> - Write a short poem or manifesto that captures your personal or cultural insights into decolonial research practices.
> - Consider what 'decolonisation' means in the context of your own research or personal experiences and how poetic inquiry can be a tool to express these concepts.

How can poetry work in research?

Poetic inquiry boasts a rich tradition (Butler-Kisber, 2002; Faulkner, 2009; Prendergast, 2009; Leavy, 2015) and encompasses various forms, such as found poetry, transcript poems, poetic transcription and research poetry. This approach transforms qualitative interview data, literary analysis and researcher reflections into poetic compositions.

As we explored in Chapter 2, poetry strives to distil complex images and experiences into concise, evocative language that encapsulates beauty, pain, questions and contradictions. Almudéver Chanzà (2021, p 1) describes poetry as both a 'reflex and reflective practice' that actively involves participants, authors and readers in a dynamic dialogue. This process starts with meticulous observation and evolves into the integration of ideas, aiming to uncover deeper meanings and insights that go beyond superficial understanding.

In the realm of research, poetry extends beyond simple theme summarisation typical of qualitative analysis. It addresses the often-criticised mechanistic approach of counting themes and codes, which can strip the human element from research findings (Rapport and Hartill, 2012). By harnessing its unique capacity to evoke and convey emotions, poetry enables a profound experiential understanding of the subject matter, bringing to life the poignant realities encountered in interviews. This not only enriches the research with nuanced emotional layers but also reconnects the audience with the visceral aspects of the topics being explored.

Researchers in Australia (Miller et al, 2015) worked with elderly residents in a care facility. They then collaborated with the acclaimed poet Sarah Holland-Batt to craft poems from the interview transcripts. Their methodology involved four crucial steps:

1. deep immersion into each transcript to extract vivid descriptions and metaphors;
2. logical organisation of these elements;
3. use of poetic techniques such as rhythm, sound and emotion;
4. refining the poems to enhance their impact.

This approach, known as 'found poetry', not only respects and honours the participants' experiences by using their actual words but also enriches the research with the expressive power of poetry. In doing so, it underscores and makes visible experiences that may have been hidden from others. A decolonial approach to poetic inquiry could also require that we take these ideas back to participants for reflection, further dialogue, refinement and co-creation of poems.

These steps offer a practical guide that you could consider adopting in your own research to harness the evocative power of poetry. Here is one poem that emerged from a research participant, called Joy.

'You could scream the place down'

My family said
I was too old
to be on my own,
that I needed organising.
You lose everything
you lose everything
to come in here.
You only have the barest minimum
There's not much here.
It is not nice, not nice at all.
It is not good for me.

I can't get out.
That's what you lose, when you come in.
All your independence is taken away from you.

The language of poetry facilitates an empathetic connection, drawing the audience into the residents' internal experiences. 'You could scream the place down' succinctly captures the dichotomy between a family's concerns over a mother's ability to manage alone and the mother's own experience of loss – loss of independence and the familiar comforts of home. Poetry juxtaposes these perspectives, providing insight into the theme of 'losing', and thus allows us to hear voices that are often disregarded or undervalued in society.

Zonke Gumede and Monde Makiwane conducted research on migration from rural to urban areas in the Eastern Cape of South Africa, a movement that often leaves family and community behind. Their poem was developed in a poetic inquiry workshop (van Rooyen and d'Abdon, 2020) and captures the emotional and social dynamics of trans-locality:

'Home'

Hopelessly overcrowded
Overworked,
Drought-stricken labour reserve,
Eroded Soil,
to live off the land
is impossible
Conditions worse
Middle Ages Serfs,
I oscillate back to the reserve,
Farm City
City
Farm
Oscillating.

Hope bright lights
glittering prizes,
low income and high cost of living.
No welcome, no chance

Keep on oscillating
Living the double life
Distances without my children
'Swing low sweet chariot, coming for to carry me home'
Life is short
Soon I'll be no more,
City Farm,
Farm Heaven

What is poetic inquiry?

Poetic inquiry is a research methodology that combines artistic expression with scientific exploration, marked by a deep curiosity and a rigorous approach to examining topics. This method involves the analysis of texts and interviews, the synthesis of information and a deep dive into understanding the words and underlying experiences of participants. Such an approach not only transforms the data but also calls into question more conventional ways of doing research and questions taken-for-granted assumptions about knowledge production. We expand on these issues in more detail in Chapter 4, but the process of engaging poetically can also profoundly affect the researcher and the ways in which we have typically engaged with our participants and our work. Researchers engaged in poetic inquiry develop a sensitivity to how traditional analysis can often simplify complex data, potentially skewing findings away from the 'flowing resonance of the raw material' (Rapport and Hartill, 2012: 19). They prioritise maintaining the richness of the story and the authenticity of the storyteller's voice over sterile analytical processes.

Using poetry as a research tool involves a commitment to capturing the essence of the participants' experiences or the phenomena under study without compromising the poetic qualities that enrich the narrative. This means that researchers must meticulously hone their craft, employing poetic sensibilities such as lines, rhythm, form, metaphor and other literary techniques to enrich their work (Butler-Kisber, 2002). This close attention to the aesthetic and critical aspects of poetry ensures that the research remains vibrant and true to the subjects' experiences, offering insights that conventional research methods might overlook.

A frequent question that we heard in the workshops we conducted for this book, was: how do we distinguish poetic inquiry from standard poetry on the same topic? Unlike merely crafting a poem, poetic inquiry involves a deeper, investigative process. To ascertain if an endeavour qualifies as poetic inquiry, consider the following key questions proposed by one of our chapter contributors, Yvonne Sliep:

1. Is there a research question guiding the creation of the poems?
2. What is the main topic being explored?
3. Has there been a review of other literature related to this topic?
4. Can the resulting poetry be appreciated as stand-alone creative work?

These questions help to clarify the intent and depth of the inquiry, ensuring that the poetic work not only serves as creative expression but also adheres to rigorous research standards. Table 3.1 highlights five key aspects that distinguish using poetic inquiry or poetry in research from composing a stand-alone poem on the same topic. We hope this aids in understanding and applying the methodology effectively.

Table 3.1: Key aspects of poetic inquiry

Aspect	Research poetry	Stand-alone poem
Purpose and context	Designed to explore and communicate research, offering a deeper understanding of the subject matter through an emotionally resonant format	Typically crafted for artistic expression and personal reflection; not constrained by the need to represent research data
Methodology	Involves a systematic process where poems are constructed from data, such as interview transcripts, field notes or other research materials, using methods like found poetry	More reliant on the poet's personal inspiration and experiences; no methodological framework tied to systematic data analysis
Engagement with data	Serves as a form of data analysis or presentation, using carefully selected words and phrases that reflect themes and nuances in the data	May draw on personal or societal experiences, but is not bound to representing systematic inquiry of data

(continued)

Table 3.1: Key aspects of poetic inquiry (continued)

Aspect	Research poetry	Stand-alone poem
Audience	Often aimed at academic or professional audiences as part of disseminating research findings; can also be used to disseminate research to wider audiences, such as the community or research participants; makes the data more accessible and is able to humanise the research so that it appeals to wider audiences	Aims at a broader audience, connecting on a personal level with readers who may share similar sentiments
Impact and use	Used to highlight emotional and subjective aspects of research data, challenging perceptions and eliciting reflective responses in ways that traditional research presentations may not	Focuses more on aesthetic appreciation and personal reflection than presenting structured research themes

Figure 3.2: Defining and mapping poetic inquiry

Exercise: defining and mapping poetic inquiry

This exercise is designed to help you deeply understand poetic inquiry by creating your own definition and visualising its components through mind-mapping.

Crafting your definition

1. Begin by thoroughly reading the section on poetic inquiry. Consider how it is differentiated from standard poetry and what unique roles it plays within research.
2. Reflect on the information you have absorbed. Write a personal definition of poetic inquiry, focusing on capturing its core essence.

Creating a mind-map

1. If you prefer a visual approach (see an example in Figure 3.2), use a mind-map to organise your thoughts. Place your definition of poetic inquiry at the centre of a large piece of paper (or you could use a digital mind-mapping tool).
2. From the central definition, draw branches that represent different aspects or dimensions of poetic inquiry. Consider including branches for:
   - Purpose: Why is poetic inquiry used in research? What does it aim to achieve?
   - Methodology: How are poetic inquiry projects typically conducted? What methods are employed?
   - Impact: What effects does poetic inquiry have on the research, its subjects and its audience?
   - Comparison with 'traditional' poetry: How does poetic inquiry use the elements of poetry differently than traditional poetic forms?

By completing this exercise, you will develop a structured and comprehensive understanding of poetic inquiry. This will not only deepen your grasp of the subject but also equip you to effectively explain and discuss this approach with others.

Next, we explore the various types of poetic inquiry you can employ in your research.

Types of poetic inquiry

Poetic inquiry is a method where poetry is employed to condense data and reinterpret it for research purposes. This technique can be applied throughout various stages of the research process, including data analysis, dissemination of results, examination of texts or literature, and reflective practice for educators or researchers. It allows for a deeper exploration of specific topics.

Generated and found poems

According to Butler-Kisber (2002), poetic inquiry can be approached in two main ways through generated and found poems.

- **Generated poems** require the researcher to compose original poems, which could be a reflective response to collected data or a personal reaction to an observed situation or idea. These poems originate from the researcher's own words and insights.
- **Found poems** are created by taking existing texts, such as participant transcripts, and transforming them into poetry. This involves selectively extracting words from sources like field notes, journal entries or other research data, and restructuring them into a poetic format.

Both are valuable for analysing and presenting data. They also serve as analytical tools that can foster deeper understanding and insights during the research process.

Generated poems

In 2022, d'Abdon published an article which used poetic inquiry as a research methodology. In it he foregrounds a decolonial interpretation of Italian playwright Carmelo Bene's misreading's of *Hamlet* and *Macbeth*. He suggests that the theatrical methods invented by Bene could possibly assist the ongoing decolonial reinvention of Shakespeare's stories in the (South) African context. The article ends with the generated poem 'shakespeare didn't work for me', which pays homage to Bene's inventiveness, originality and defiant spirit.

'shakespeare didn't work for me'

until i hit my thirties

too many unschooled teachers telling me
how damn good he was and

too many insipid
hollywood versions
of his stuff

i found
the sonnets honeyed and
to be or not to be that is the question
the wackest line ever
(i still do)

reading him was like
strolling in fog-wrapped
sunflower fields

and it took an italian buffoon
to pull the bard's soul out of the page
and unlock the magic

his grunts and ululations
his screams and contortions
blew the fog away

and the mad kings
the cunning queens
the wise fools

the blind earls
the smart witches
the horny heiresses
the doomed lovers
the insolent monsters
the airy spirits
and the vengeful ghosts
popped up one by one
tap-dancing on the sunflower

now i'm in my late forties
and he works just fine

i even like the sonnets

Exercise: developing a generated poem

In this exercise, you'll reflect on deep emotional and relational themes presented in quotes by bell hooks (2000) from her book *All About Love*. Choose one of the following quotes as a starting point for a free-flow writing session:

> When we face pain in relationships our first response is often to sever bonds rather than to maintain commitment.

> For me, forgiveness and compassion are always linked: how do we hold people accountable for wrongdoing and yet at the same time remain in touch with their humanity enough to believe in their capacity to be transformed?

1. Begin by free writing for 10 minutes in response to the quote you selected. Allow any thoughts, words, phrases or sentences to flow without judgment, focusing on the ideas expressed in the quote.

2. After your writing session, review what you have written and underline words or phrases that resonate with you or stand out in some way.

3. Write each of the words or phrases you have underlined on separate strips of paper.

4. Randomly select one of these strips of paper. Use the selected word or phrase as a prompt to initiate another free writing session for five minutes.

5. From this second session, again choose standout words or phrases and write them on new strips of paper. You should have about eight strips now.

6. Rearrange these strips into a sequence that feels coherent or powerful to you, forming a poem from these elements.

Found poems

In this section, we discuss a few examples of found poems generated from texts and research data.

In an enlightening essay published in the *Johannesburg Review of Books*, South African poet and scholar Makhosazana Xaba (2018) outlines her method for creating found poems from Mohale Mashigo's 2016 novel *The Yearning*. Xaba not only shares the poems but also provides a meticulous guide to her process, enhancing transparency and reproducibility for anyone interested in her technique. She explains that 'the first number indicates the page on Mashigo's novel and the second number shows the exact line on the page from which the words were taken. This way, anyone interested in examining the original text will be able to find the words with ease' (Xaba, 2018).

This approach showcases the meticulous attention to detail required in found poetry, where the origin of each phrase is crucial to both the poem's integrity and its connection to the source material. Xaba used the same method with Barbara Boswell's 2017 novel *Grace*. The found poems created out of it are published in the collection *The Art of Waiting for Tales: A Collection of Poems Found in Grace: A Novel*, by Barbara Boswell, published by Lukhanyo Publishers in 2022. The example poem, 'Yearning', is a demonstration of Xaba's method.

'Yearning (1.title)'

> The yearning haunts (1.12) mother (1.12)
> Hurts (1.14) the life in me (1.14)
> A (1.15) part (1.16) has vanished (1.16)
> I'm (1.16) faced with (1.16) possibilities. (1.17)
> The yearning (1.17) brought us here
> In our quiet denial. (1.18)

Here are some of Xaba's notes on how she worked:

- Found in the chapter, 'The Yearning', page 5, lines 12–18.
- I found the title of the poem from the title of the opening chapter of the novel without the 'the'.
- In instances where I found words in the same line but where they were separated by other words – as is the case with the opening line – I demonstrate this by inserting the reference where the separating words appear.

In a 2022 article, 'Slam to heal: a poetic inquiry reflection', d'Abdon develops found poems from interviews with poets on their experiences with slam poetry. Initially presented as snippets scattered throughout the article, these poetic excerpts were eventually compiled into a single, cohesive poem, showcasing a collective narrative on the impact of slam poetry (van Rooyen et al, 2023).

'to slam or not to slam?'

1.
posture poets
legislate for others
yet know nothing of
motsapi

*nyezwa
muila
dladla*

*in their own world
poetry started with them*

*2.
slam jam
mimic thugs
ignore rich voices*

*celebrities worshipped by
government and corporate*

*3.
radical shamans
at the top of the big stage
warriors who recite with precision
truly brilliant writers*

*4.
in the gladiator arena
poetry is not what matters*

performance is in the spotlight

*slam is cheapened
kind of writing*

*5.
undoing my silence
my journey of healing*

*speaking out does help me dealing with depression
and stress*

*poems to the child I was
the child crying now*

> *cry child, cry*
> *it is a way of healing*

Three types of voice in research poems

Prendergast (2009) categorises research poems into three primary types based on their sources, which she terms *voxes* (voices): **researcher-voiced, participant-voiced, and literature-voiced poems**. Each type can employ either found or generated poetry methods, depending on whether the poem is created from existing texts or newly written by the researcher.

Vox theoria *(literature-voiced poems)*

These poems are based on literary or theoretical texts. For example, Heidi van Rooyen (2024) employed poetic inquiry while reviewing contemporary literature on the topic of the 'end of AIDS and post-AIDS'. During her review, she identified several recurrent themes:

- the oversimplification of complex social realities by language;
- the necessity to include the voices of people living with HIV and AIDS;
- the intersection of HIV and AIDS with social inequalities;
- the influence of social and structural issues on HIV prevention;
- the need for radical interdisciplinarity in addressing these issues.

Van Rooyen crafted found poems for each theme, transforming the dense theoretical discourse into accessible and reflective poetic works. Here is an example of a found poem she developed from the literature she reviewed:

> *the embodied*
> *everyday sense*
> *of risk,*
> *the daily tasks*
> *of living with*
> *HIV and AIDS,*
> *its stigma*

the uncertainty
anxiety
the economic drain
and social tumble
through life
with an illness
with no cure
this story
my story
our story
silenced
by your
post-AIDS talk

Vox autobiographia/autoethnographia *(researcher-voiced poems)*

This category consists of researcher-voiced poems that stem from personal data sources such as field notes, journal entries, or reflective and autobiographical writings. These poems are deeply self-reflective, often exploring the researcher's own experiences and insights.

For example, Yvonne Sliep (2012) uses an autoethnographic approach to explore her grief and loss after her son's death. She details four years of her grieving process, intertwining her reflective writing with her experiences of loss and support during this time. Sliep enriches the article with poems she wrote at pivotal moments – the first one at the onset of her grief and the other a month later. These poems, 'In Taiwan' and 'One month', act as expressive waypoints in her journey, showcasing the power of poetic inquiry to articulate profound personal experiences deeply and meaningfully. In the process and practice of writing, the author gains useful insights (and perhaps healing) and, through her words, then engages the reader in a similar co-inquiry about these topics.

'In Taiwan'

the fridge door is opened
his body rolled out
without a word
the bag unzipped

it has been days
but his body is unwashed
his torn clothes have his smell
on his face a peaceful smile
sculpted in wax
stubbles on his handsome face
I kiss his frozen lips

'One month'

every day I break a little less
but what is gone does not come back
my tears create pathways
to find a different life
another identity
my deep motherly love
could not protect him enough in this life
and now he is the one that looks over me

Sliep (2012) uses herself as a subject to gain understanding about grief, thus using her professional psychology background and poetic inquiry to reflect on her deeply personal experience and, later, to share some of it to 'help' others and offer alternatives to dominant discourses about grief. The writing offers a reflexive dialogical space of exploring her own experience, but in dialogue with the reader and her son.

Vox participare *(participant-based poems)*

These poems originate from the voices of participants, typically drawn from interview transcripts or directly solicited contributions. They may be crafted solely by the participants or co-created with the researcher, and can incorporate either individual or collective participant voices. This approach often blends the voices of both the researcher and the participants to deepen the narrative.

For instance, in a collaborative effort by Sliep and colleagues (2024), a poem was co-created during the research process. Here, the researcher echoed back the words she heard from a participant during an interview and, together, they shaped these reflections into a poem. This method not only captures the participant's voice but also actively involves them in the expression of their own experiences, illustrating the interactive and inclusive nature of poetic inquiry.

lots of bodies moving around chaotically
bad blood amongst all of us
and nowhere at all to go to
violence sparks grudges and jealousy
and nowhere at all to go to
first my father was stabbed
six times in the chest
the day six cows were slaughtered
to change the wrath
of the ancestors
then my brother was stabbed
five times in the back
all in the name of envy
punished because he dared
to go to varsity
I know
I am next in line
I know
it is coming
I too go to varsity
I do not know
who I am
I do not know
where I want to go to
I know it has to be away from here

Later, Prendergast (2015) identified additional categories of voices in poetic inquiry, reflecting broader applications and deeper understandings within (post-)qualitative research. Although, for simplicity, these categories are not detailed here, those interested are encouraged to consult the original references for more in-depth exploration. Identifying with one of these voices can help clarify the primary aim of your poetic inquiry and sharpen the focus of your research. Having explored types of poems, we turn next to the practicalities of how to implement this methodology.

How to create research poems

Creating research poems is a transformative process that can be approached in various ways. We discussed a four-step method employed by a research team in Australia earlier in this chapter. Here, we explore another set of guidelines, developed by van Rooyen and d'Abdon (2020) in their comprehensive paper on converting research data into poetic forms, which also draws from the methods of several other researchers engaged in poetic inquiry.

Creating research poems

1. **Data collection:** Begin with gathering qualitative data, which be from interviews, focus groups, field notes or any other relevant data sources. For example, conducting semi-structured interviews is a common method for capturing rich, detailed accounts of participants' experiences.
2. **Immersive reading:** Thoroughly read through the collected data multiple times to immerse yourself in the details and nuances of the content. This deep engagement helps to identify vivid descriptions, emotional undertones and significant metaphors that can be used in your poems. This reading may be done with a decolonial lens, looking for the marginalised or hidden voice; this could be done collaboratively with participants in co-creation with an awareness of power, dynamics and voice.
3. **Thematic coding:** Code the data to organise and categorise the information (Faulkner, 2009; Leavy, 2015). This might involve inductively developing codes from the data, identifying patterns and themes.
4. **Highlighting of themes:** You can identify and record recurring themes or concepts that appear across the data set. For example, in research on motherhood, themes might include 'love and worry', 'willingness to give' and 'resenting the sacrifice'. This step is crucial to distil the essence of the data into manageable parts for poetic transcription.
5. **Extraction of key phrases:** Extract key phrases and snippets that strongly represent the themes, or convey the core sentiments, of

your data. Begin shaping these extracts into a poetic format, carefully considering the flow and emotional impact of the words.

6. **Condensation:** Remove superfluous words and rearrange segments to distil the themes more crisply.
7. **Textual arrangement:** Work with chunks of text, rearranging sentences or phrases to juxtapose words and short phrases against each other, enhancing the thematic portrayal.
8. **Poetic licence:** Rearrange words, use pauses and adjust line lengths to intensify the poem's meaning. Remember some of the tools and techniques you read about in Chapter 2. See if you can use poetic devices such as the 3 Rs (rhythm, rhyme and repetition) to enhance the poem's lyrical quality. Can you pick up metaphors, similes and figures of speech. Can they be retained and used? These aspects of craft not only make the emerging poem more engaging but also help to convey the depth of the data in a resonant way.
9. **Iteration and refinement:** Continuously refine your poem, experimenting with different arrangements of lines and stanzas to find the most powerful expression of the data. This may involve adding or removing words, adjusting line breaks or playing with the overall structure of the poem.
10. **Feedback and revision:** Read the poem aloud to test its rhythmic flow and ensure it sounds natural and coherent. Share your poem with others, ideally including participants, if possible, to get feedback. Does the poem resonate with their experience? What tweaks or adjustments need to be made so that the poem is most reflective of their realities? How will participants be acknowledged in the work? This co-creation between researcher and participants, challenges conventional norms about how we do research; it honours participant voices, and it places the power to craft and create in both sets of hands. These decolonial practices can result in poems that speak vividly to the lived realities of others and that are capable of resonating with others.
11. **Finalisation:** Decide whether the poem will be published. While not all poems need to be published, the process of writing them is invaluable for exploring and elucidating research themes. This step often involves ensuring that the poem aligns with ethical guidelines, particularly in terms of participant confidentiality and the accurate representation of experiences (we pick this up again in Chapter 4).

Three examples of steps we have taken to develop found poems on various research projects are presented next.

Example 1: A study on homelessness in South Africa

Here is an extract from the study on homelessness:

> I am from [a place in Kwazulu-Natal] that's where my brothers are. I was with relatives here .... While I was staying with my relatives it came to a point where I could feel that they did not want me there anymore, you know? I just came to Durban. I have no mother, I have no father, my father passed away when I was very young, I was just moving from here to there, renting at people's homes. I have no one. My one child passed away, and my brothers have all passed away. I am the only one left, with my one child; and this one Zulu where I was renting, I was running around, renting and my child left me there. And so I found a place in the informal settlements. I was living there in the shacks, renting, paying rent. Now, I am paying rent then my child was just crying the whole time, that's when I came to Durban. I have been living in the streets of Durban for five years. I go beg at the [mosque], then I use the money to buy food then I sleep on the floor at night.

This is the found poem developed:

> 'I have no one'
>
> *I was staying with my relatives*
> *They did not want me anymore*
> *I came to Durban*
>
> *I have no mother*
> *I have no father*
> *I was just moving*
> *here and there*
> *I have no one*

> *My one child passed away*
> *my brothers have all passed away*
> *I am the only one left with my one child*
> *I was running around*
> *and my child left me*
> *I found a place in the informal settlements*
> *I was living in the shacks*
> *I have no one*
>
> *I have been living in the streets for five years*
> *I go beg*
> *I use the money to buy food*
> *I sleep on the floor at night*
> *I have no one*

The words highlighted in bold italics in the next paragraph indicate the exact words used to generate the found poem.

> I am from [a place in Kwazulu-Natal] that's where my brothers are. I was with relatives here ... . While ***I was staying with my relatives*** it came to a point where I could feel that ***they did not want me there anymore***, you know? I just came to Durban. ***I have no mother, I have no father***, my father passed away when I was very young, ***I was just moving from here to there***, renting at people's homes. ***I have no one***. ***My one child passed away***, and my brothers have all passed away. I am the only one left, with my one child; and this one Zulu where I was renting. ***I was running around***, renting and my child left me there. And so I found a place in the informal settlements. ***I was living there in the shacks***, renting, paying rent. Now, I am paying rent then my child was just crying the whole time, that's when I came to Durban. ***I have been living in the streets*** of Durban ***for five years***. I go beg at the [mosque], then ***I use the money to buy food*** then ***I sleep on the floor at night***.

As you can see, extra words are cut out, certain phrases are distilled and ordered, and the poem reads with a real impact and remains

Poetic Inquiry as Research

true to the speaker's words. This method of poetic inquiry not only preserves the voice and experiences of the participants but also enhances the impact of their stories by presenting them in a format that is accessible and poignant. Through poetry, complex emotions and subtleties of human experiences are conveyed effectively, providing insights that might be overlooked in traditional research presentations.

Example 2: Exploring trans identities in Namibia

In Table 3.2, the column on the left contains a transcript from one of the interviews with trans women in Namibia (see van Rooyen et al, 2021). The poem is constructed using the highlighted key words from the column to the right. These words form the backbone of the poem, weaving the participants' experiences into a coherent and emotionally resonant narrative.

In this example, the poet-researcher skilfully employs the participants' exact words, refining and arranging them to enhance their impact through the use of poetic techniques, notably repetition. The careful selection and repetitive use

Table 3.2: Exploring trans identities in Namibia: verbatim and poetic transcription

Verbatim transcript in dialogue	Poetic transcription (taking out phrases from the original transcript)
At Eveline street, **nobody is safe, especially** for **trans women, you** will **stand there, have your fun, have your beer,** all of a sudden **a dude just comes and kicks you** up **for no reason, you did nothing**. He beats you. Nobody will help you, they will stand and stare at you. … And **nobody, nobody, nobody** at all will help you, they will stand and they will stare at you until everything is done. The person can even kill you there, they will just stand and look at you till the guy is done with you.	nobody is safe, especially trans women, you stand there, have your fun, have your beer, a dude just comes, and kicks you for no reason. you did nothing. … They will kill you Nobody Nobody Nobody Will help you. They stand and stare until the guy is done.

of specific phrases underscore significant points, making the poem not only a reflection of real sentiments but also a powerful resonant piece that invites readers to engage deeply with the content.

Example 3: Using poetry to explore motherhood

Angela is considering writing on her subjective experience of motherhood for an upcoming conference. This example illustrates the creative mind-mapping process she uses to brainstorm, organise and then distil her thoughts about motherhood.

Process of poetic creation:

- Angela places her hand a on blank piece of paper and traces the shape around her hand and fingers.
- Each finger represents a different dimension or element of her experience as a mother, such as nurturing, disciplining, loving, worrying and balancing work and home life.
- A central theme or title of the poem is placed in the palm of the hand. Angela then selects words and phrases that resonate with each element, using them as a foundation to construct her poems (see Figure 3.3).

Poetic techniques used:

- The poem uses vivid imagery and emotive language to convey the complexities of motherhood.
- Angela incorporates the poetic device of repetition to emphasise certain aspects of her experience, echoing the cyclical and ongoing nature of maternal duties.

'Motherhood'

*Is lived above ground
In daily tasks
Tick tick look at the clock
Who is going where
At what time*

Figure 3.3: Angela Hough's mind-map

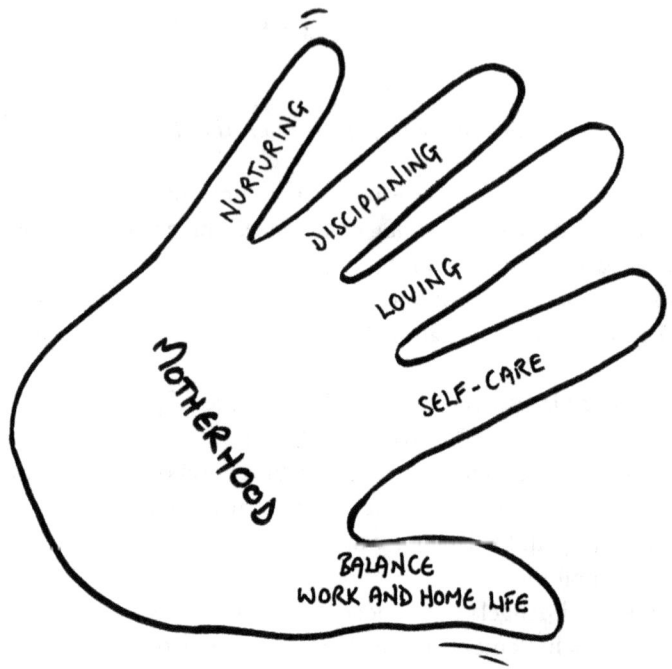

Lunch boxes
Breakfast bowls
Load the dishwasher
The daily hustle
Tick tock look
At the clock

Is lived below ground
In the dreamscape
Where tree roots meet
Weaving dreams of hope
Wrangling fears and worries.
In the emotional labour of love
And the unconscious realms
of how we were mothered.

Is lived
In the spaces in-between:
Between work and home;
Between lover and mother;
Between Self and other
Between child and mother
Between an neglect and smother
In the balance of self-sacrifice and self- care.
Is lived in relation
to each child's unfolding path
and the inter-weaving inter-section
with your path
and the contexts you live in.

And feels not enough
When I have done so much.

By reflecting on her personal journey through poetry, Angela invites readers to connect with the universal aspects of motherhood, offering a window into the intimate and often unspoken challenges and joys of being a mother. The researcher could develop the poems into a fuller poetic auto-ethnography. Auto-ethnography is a methodology where researchers use their personal experiences to understand cultural, social or personal phenomena (Holman-Jones et al, 2013). The poems that emerge could be a starting point for an engagement with similar themes in the scholarly literature on mothering and motherhood. This back and forth, between the poems and the literature, could help the author deepen and analyse both the poems, and her subjective experience of motherhood. Such an approach demonstrates how poetry can serve as a powerful medium for expressing and understanding the nuances of the broader social and cultural experience of motherhood, thus bridging the gap between subjective experience and academic inquiry.

We have given you several examples and illustrations of how it is possible to work with research data and turn them into poems. Now it is your turn! Everyone has a unique story to tell and, while some choose to express themselves through essays, novels, songs or plays, others find poetry to be the most effective medium.

Like any skill, writing poetry requires practice. Initially, it might feel challenging, but regular practice can significantly enhance your abilities. Eventually, writing poetry can become second nature, where the mechanics of it flow effortlessly.

We have detailed one methodology for transforming data into poetry, as developed by van Rooyen and d' Abdon (2020) and Faulkner (2019). In the box on the three-step method, we introduce a more concise approach. You could take some of your own research data and apply one of these approaches to start your journey into poetic inquiry.

The three-step method

Step 1: The three-read

Read your working material (data, interviews, articles in progress and so on) *three times*

1. Read to get a general impression of the material at your disposal (get an overview)
2. Read to identify and locate keywords and potential figurative language (beautiful images, metaphors, similes, allusions and so on) (look at details)
3. Read to figure out what the 'hidden' story is in the data at your disposal. What is this chaotic material trying to tell you? What might be a thread or storyline or juxtaposition or polarity in the key themes? (synthesise) Perhaps something is not being said? What is the hidden message? What is your position as researcher? What are the voices of participants? What dynamics of power are at play? Poems can bring to light (or not ignore) intersections of race, gender and sexuality and reflect on hidden or marginalised stories or paradoxes. Can you make these systemic barriers visible through the poem?

Step 2: Choose keywords for your research poem:

Now you should begin selecting effective keywords. Think of them as the 'skeleton' of your poem.

1. Read through your data and highlight any key terms or phrases that are most relevant to the focus of your work. Highlight evocative phrases.
2. Draw up a shortlist of those that capture your sense of the data.

Step 3: Write your research poem

Think of:

- Intro (opening line or first stanza)
  Bring the main topic of your research to life. This could include a metaphor or comparison.
- Body (central stanzas)
  Build your argument or describe the context.
  Poetry helps the audience feel with the person or people, and places, you are representing. Giving some context assists this. Poetry hopefully helps us discover something about ourselves or the world. We learn something or are reminded about the human condition and ourselves.
- Conclusion (closing line or final stanza)
  This is a summary insight or a juxtaposition (counterpoint or multiple voice).

Now explore poetic methods such as simile, metaphor and repetition of lines or sounds to add to the craft of your poem. Recall what we covered in Chapter 2.

Read your poem out loud and edit. Sometimes it helps to sit with a poem for a few days. Creating poems from data is not just a linear process but one of taking fragments, a 'mental kaleidoscope' of insights, gathering and synthesising, and creating a poem which offers insight into the experience.

Exercise: reflecting on poetic inquiry

As we wrap up this chapter on poetic inquiry, we encourage you to engage in a personal reflection to consolidate your understanding and consider the implications of this approach. Please contemplate the following questions and jot down your thoughts:

1. What are your thoughts on the different types of poems used in poetic inquiry, such as generated poems and found poems?

2. Reflect on the process of transforming data into poetry. What would you find challenging or exciting? Consider both the creative and analytical elements of this method.

3. Where and how could you envision applying poetic inquiry in your professional or personal projects? Think about specific contexts or topics where this method could enhance understanding or expression.

Take your time to reflect on the questions in the last exercise. It is not only about understanding poetic inquiry but also about discovering how it can be integrated into your own research and creative endeavours.

Conclusion

We hope this chapter has provided you with valuable insights into writing research poems. Our aim was to demonstrate how poetic inquiry can offer a fresh perspective on research data, fostering empathy and deeper understanding of participants' experiences through multiple voices. Poetic inquiry marries the 'researcher gaze' with the 'aesthetic/artist/poet gaze' (Gill and Waters, 2009), combining scientific rigour with literary creativity to satisfy the dual identity of scientist and poet inherent in researchers.

In the upcoming chapter, we delve into what constitutes a 'good research poem'. This includes adhering to truthfulness and reflective accuracy concerning the data while also enhancing the aesthetic appeal of the poetry created. We discuss the ethical considerations of poetic inquiry and its decolonial potential. Denzin and Lincoln (1994) highlight the importance of legitimation and representation – choices about what and who to include, how stories are told and who gets to access them can significantly shape research outcomes.

As we continue, we will explore criteria that help determine whether a research poem is 'good enough'. Here's to a journey that not only enlightens but also inspires.

References

Akomolafe, B. (2018) 'Times are urgent, so let us slow down', *YouTube*, available at: www.youtube.com/watch?v=bBVAYzBteIo

Almudéver Chanzà, J. (2021) *(Re)inventions and (Dis)continuations of the Catholic Tradition: Community-Making in a Spanish Village*, PhD thesis, University of Edinburgh.

Boswell, B. (2017) *Grace*, Cape Town: Modjaji.

Butler-Kisber, L. (2002) 'Artful portrayals in qualitative inquiry: the road to found poetry and beyond', *Alberta Journal of Educational Research*, 48(3). doi: 10.11575/ajer.v48i3.54930

d'Abdon, R. (2022) 'Slam to heal: a poetic inquiry reflection', *Le Simplegadi*, XX: 105–21.

d'Abdon, R. (2023) 'To slam or not to slam?', in H. van Rooyen (ed) *Voices Unbound: Poems of the Eighth International Symposium on Poetic Inquiry*, Cape Town: African Sun Press, pp 51–2.

Dalal, F. (2014) 'Ethics versus compliance: the institution, ethical psychotherapy', *Group Analysis*, 47(1): 62–81.

Denzin, N.K. and Lincoln, Y.S. (eds) (1994) *Handbook of Qualitative Research*, London: Sage.

Faulkner, S. (2009) *Poetry as Method*, Walnut Creek, CA: Left Coast Press.

Faulkner, S.L. (2019) *Poetic Inquiry: Craft, Method and Practice*, London: Routledge.

Gill, J. and Waters, M. (2009) 'Poetry and autobiography', *Life Writing*, 6(1): 1–9.

Holman-Jones, S.L., Adams, T.E. and Ellis, C. (2013) *Handbook of Autoethnography*, Walnut Creek, CA: Left Coast Press.

hooks, b. (2000/2018) *All About Love: New Visions*, New York: William Morrow Publishers.

Kaunda, C.J and Fubah, M.A. (2023) '"I am gay"', in Heidi van Rooyen (ed) *Voices Unbound: Poems of the Eighth International Symposium on Poetic Inquiry*, Cape Town: African Sun Press and HSRC.

Leavy, P. (2015) *Method Meets Art: Arts Based Research Practice*, New York: Guilford Press.

Letters Live (2023) 'Stephen Fry reads Nick Cave's stirring letter about ChatGPT and human creativity', *YouTube*, available at: www.youtube.com/watch?v=iGJcF4bLKd4

Miller, E., Donoghue, G. and Holland-Batt, S. (2015) '"You could scream the place down": five poems on the experience of aged care', *Qualitative Inquiry*, 21(5): 410–17.

Prendergast, M. (2009) in M. Prendergast, C. Leggo and P. Sameshima (eds) *Poetic Inquiry: Vibrant Voices in the Social Sciences*, Rotterdam: Sense Publishers.

Prendergast, M. (2015) 'Poetic inquiry, 2007–2012: a surrender and catch found poem', *Qualitative Inquiry*, 21(8): 678–85.

Rapport, F. and Harthill, G. (2012) 'Crossing disciplines with ethnographic poetic representation', *Creative Approaches to Research*, 5: 11–15.

Richardson, L. (2002) 'Poetic representation of interviews', in J. Gubrium and J. Holstein (eds), *Handbook of Interview Research*, Thousand Oaks, California: Sage, pp 877–91.

Sibiya, A.T. and Ndaba, M. (2023) 'Moving from discourse to praxis: situating academics at the centre of the decolonisation struggle', *South African Journal of Higher Education*, 37(3): 214-28.

Sliep, Y. (2012). 'We compose our own requiem. An autoethnographic study of mourning', *Creative Approaches to Research*, 5(2): 61-85.

Sliep, Y., Makhakhe, N.F., Ngcongo, S. and Calmes, B. (2022) 'Working with life stories for transformational learning: tracking our positionality in an educational dialogical space during COVID-19', in C. Kagan, R. Lawthom, A.X.Z. Zambrano, J.A.A. Inzunza, M. Richards and J. Akhurst (eds) *The Routledge International Handbook of Community Psychology: Facing Global Crises with Hope*, London: Routledge, pp 355–70.

Sliep, Y., Norton, L., Naidu, T. and Makhakhe, N.F. (2024) 'Levelling the field in PhD super-vision: a polyvocal journey of poemish inquiry', in H. van Rooyen and Kathleen Pithouse-Morgan (eds) *Poetic Inquiry for the Human and Social Sciences: Voices from the South and North*, Cape Town: HSRC Press, pp 213–27.

van Rooyen, H. (ed) (2023) *Voices Unbound: Poems of the Eighth International Symposium on Poetic Inquiry*, Cape Town: African Sun Press.

van Rooyen, H. (2024) 'A poetic inquiry: the role of the social sciences and humanities in revitalising AIDS', *AIDS* Care, 36(supp. 1): 223–27. doi: 10.1080/09540121.2024.2319840. Epub 2024 Feb. 23. PMID: 38394381.

van Rooyen, H. and d'Abdon, R. (2020) 'Transforming data into poems: poetic inquiry practices for social and human sciences', *Education as Change*, 24(1): 1–17.

van Rooyen, H. and Pithouse-Morgan, K. (eds) (2024) *Poetic Inquiry for the Human and Social Sciences: Voices from the South and North*, Cape Town: HSRC Press.

van Rooyen, H., Essack, Z., Mahali, A., Groenewald, C. and Solomons, A. (2021) '"The power of the poem": using poetic inquiry to explore trans-identities in Namibia', *Arts and Health*, 13(3): 315–28.

Xaba, M. (2018) 'Found poems by Makhosazana Xaba, from Mohale Mashigo's novel "The Yearning"', *The Johannesburg Review of Books*, 15 January, available at: https://johannesburgreviewofbooks.com/2018/01/15/conversation-issue-found-poems-by-makhosazana-xaba-from-mohale-mashigos-novel-the-yearning/

4

Navigating ethical territories in poetic inquiry

Yvonne Sliep, Angela Hough and Duduzile S. Ndlovu

This chapter addresses the ethical aspects of poetic inquiry, focusing on power, decolonisation and critical reflexivity. It includes exercises to develop reflexivity, thereby increasing the ethical rigour of research. The discussion extends to inclusive representation, visibility of power structures and the use of poetic inquiry for social justice. We challenge conventional mappings of knowledge and encourage a revaluation of whose experiences are highlighted, promoting a deeper exploration of identity through poetry.

Introduction

Using poetic devices in research introduces an innovative and creative dimension that emphasises the 'voice' in research narratives. This approach allows for a nuanced exploration of complex human experiences, often extending beyond the confines of 'Euro-Western' academic discourse. Researchers are encouraged to maintain a close connection to context and integrate this thoughtfully into their poems to authentically represent their findings.

However, it is crucial to uphold ethical rigour throughout the research process, even when using creative methodologies such as poetic inquiry. Key ethical considerations include adhering to research principles such as informed consent, anonymity, beneficence, respecting participants' voices and stories, ensuring confidentiality and accurately representing their experiences and perspectives. This heightened ethical awareness is necessary because transforming research data into poetry can sometimes alter or obscure the original meanings and experiences of the participants. Only the participants themselves can validate the authenticity of their represented stories.

Moreover, research is inherently filled with power dynamics that require careful navigation, particularly regarding the researcher's position. This power, often rooted in institutional affiliations and social markers such as economic status, race, gender and age, significantly influences the interactions between researchers and participants. In contexts committed to a decolonial agenda, such as in Africa, it is vital to confront and dismantle the colonial legacies embedded in research methodologies. This demands a critical revaluation and disruption of the colonial gaze by including creative methods (Chilisa, 2012; Pedri-Spade, 2016), promoting a more equitable and reflective research practice.

Poetic inquiry challenges us to critically assess not only the map – representing the framework and perspective of our research – but also the territory it purports to describe. We are prompted to question whose perspectives are prioritised, whose are marginalised and how these choices shape our understanding. Through this inquiry, we strive to flip conventional narratives, exploring and understanding ourselves and our identities through our writing and the intersectionalities these reveal. This approach not only shifts how we view the subject matter but also underscores the importance of understanding ethical research principles and power dynamics, essential for responsible qualitative research.

Understanding power dynamics in ethical research

In research involving human subjects, it is essential to understand and articulate your *positionality* – how your social, economic or educational status influences interactions with participants. This concept, known as positionality (Alcott, 1988), highlights the need to recognise and navigate the power dynamics inherent in these relationships. Researchers are encouraged to critically evaluate their own biases and assumptions to avoid distorting the data with preconceived notions or simplistic binary views (Sliep et al, 2021).

When conducting qualitative research, particularly through poetic inquiry, ethical considerations are crucial to maintain the integrity and authenticity of the research process. These considerations are particularly important when addressing the power dynamics inherent in the research relationship.

Principles of ethical research

- Respect the autonomy of participants.
- Beneficence: Who is the research for? Who does it serve? (This is illustrated in Figure 4.1.)
- Even if it is in poetry, the research still has to be valid.
- Poetic inquiry expresses both the inside and the outside story.
- The context of the research has to be visible.

Figure 4.1: Who does the research serve?

Here is how these principles are applied:

1. **Respecting participant autonomy:** This involves ensuring informed consent, which includes providing clear information about the purpose of the research, its uses and measures to protect participant privacy and identity. In poetic inquiry, where poems may consist solely of participants' words, it is essential to discuss who will be credited as the author of the poem – whether it will be the participant, the researcher or both. This discussion should ideally be part of the initial consent negotiation, ensuring that participants understand and agree on how their contributions and authorship are represented.

2. **Beneficence:** Researchers must continuously reflect on who benefits from the research. Discussions with participants should clarify the intended benefits and outcomes of the research, prioritising participant needs and perspectives. Questions about who benefits from the research, how they benefit and who has access to the information should be addressed transparently. If naming participants poses risks, using pseudonyms can be a balanced approach, provided it is discussed and agreed on with the participants.
3. **Validity:** Ensuring the validity of research findings involves staying truthful to the data collected through interviews and observations. Poetic inquiry, acknowledging the subjective lenses of both the researcher and the participants, emphasises the importance of transparency regarding the researcher's biases and perspectives. This approach involves listening to and amplifying non-dominant voices and checking with participants to confirm the accuracy and resonance of the findings.
4. **Inside and outside perspective:** Our social identities often become rigidly defined through the 'gaze' of others, which sees us from the outside in. To avoid merely recounting an outsider's perspective in our research, it is vital to integrate the rich, nuanced insider's viewpoint. This is where poetic inquiry proves invaluable, as it aims to express the 'inside and outside story' in a way that fosters deeper understanding.
5. **Context:** By using poetic techniques, we can avoid reducing human identities to stereotypes, projections or assumptions, instead highlighting their complex, nuanced realities. Poetic narratives, which are a crucial part of qualitative research, occur within a specific 'context'. Understanding this context enriches our interpretation of participant stories and enhances the potential for fostering social justice.

By incorporating these ethical principles, poetic inquiry not only respects the rights of participants but also enriches the research process, making it more inclusive and reflective of diverse human experiences. In addition, it renders visibility and dignity (Sliep, 2012). Through this methodology, researchers can more effectively navigate the complexities of social identities and power dynamics, offering a richer, more nuanced portrayal of participant stories.

This ethical rigour ensures that the poetic narratives crafted are not only compelling but also just and respectful to the individuals whose experiences they depict.

In the poem 'Own my life today', the poet-researcher delves into her own experiences with power dynamics, reflecting on how these forces shape perceptions and interactions within the research context. This introspective piece serves as an exploration of both the overt and subtle influences that power exerts on the researcher's work and identity, providing a personal narrative that underscores the themes discussed in this chapter.

'Own my life today'

Let me tell my story
What I own in this world
Is the word
It creates and destroys
It is power
Let me build castles
crown kings and queens
warriors and heroes
My mothers, sisters
brothers and fathers
will be
Let me paint a picture
heavy and light strokes
my words will paint
the blue expanse
wittingly covered
by the shimmering night-tide
Let me use my words
borrow your language
so you can hear but
tell my own story
for my children to hear
Let me claim the
power on my tongue to
trace my past
chart my path

define my name
Own my life
Will you listen?

The first exercise in this chapter, on the power of power, is designed to help you engage deeply with the themes of power as discussed in the poem 'Own my life today'. This reflective writing prompt encourages a personal exploration of the poem's impact on your understanding of power dynamics and guides you through creating your own poetic response.

Exercise: the power of power

1. Carefully read 'Own my life today'. Reflect on its themes and the emotions it evokes about power dynamics.

2. Choose three lines from the poem that particularly resonate with you. These lines should speak powerfully to your own experiences or insights regarding power.

3. Free writing session:
   - Spend two minutes free writing about the first line you chose. Let your thoughts flow without editing them.
   - Next, take the second line you chose and write freely for another two minutes. Explore the thoughts and feelings this line brings up.
   - Finally, use the last selected line to inspire a further two minutes of free writing.

4. Create your poem:
   - After completing your free writing sessions, read over your text. Underline any sentences or phrases that stand out to you.
   - Craft these selected lines into a poem. Arrange them in a way that feels coherent and impactful to you. This poem should reflect your personal interpretation of and reaction to the theme of power.

5. Share and reflect:
   - If possible, share your poem with someone else – it may be a fellow researcher, a friend or a group. Discuss what you've written and what you've learned.
   - Reflect on what you've noticed about power that stands out to you. How does it influence your view of the poem and its application to your life or work?

This exercise not only deepens your engagement with the poem but also enhances your understanding of how power dynamics can be reflected and explored through poetry. It provides an opportunity to use poetic expression as a means of introspection and discussion.

Applying ethics in poetic inquiry

To conclude this section on ethical frameworks guiding poetic inquiry, we focus on procedural ethics and the ethics of practice that shape our research conduct.

Procedural ethics involve formal protocols overseen by academic or research institutions, which act as gatekeepers to ensure ethical research practices. This includes obtaining informed consent from all participants, guaranteeing confidentiality and upholding anonymity where required. It also thoroughly details how participants are protected throughout the research process and how transparency will be maintained in all actions. Ethics committees evaluate these procedures based on the qualifications and experience of the research team. The researcher's personal approach can significantly influence the dynamics of the research.

Ethics of practice refers to the ethical dilemmas that occur daily throughout the research process. These highlight the disparity between check box-oriented procedural ethics and the more intricate, nuanced practice of ethics in real-world research settings. Researchers must carefully navigate the grey areas within and beyond official ethical guidelines, always from the perspective of the research participants (Hopkins, 2015). For example, researchers are required to act on any discovery of harm, such as instances of abuse, which, by law, must be reported (Orb et al, 2001).

Implementing ethical practices in poetic inquiry goes beyond mere compliance with rules. It demands an engaged, reflective approach to the ethical dimensions of research, consistently evaluating how one's position and the power dynamics at play affect every phase of the project, from gathering data to analysis and dissemination of results. By integrating reflexivity and stringent ethical standards, researchers ensure their work is academically robust and, at the same time, represents the voices and experiences of participants respectfully and accurately.

We have examined the foundational ethical principles that guide responsible research, including how to handle issues of power inherent in the research process. Next, we turn our focus to understanding subjectivity and reflexivity and their critical role in research. Reflexivity involves a continuous awareness of one's influence on the research and its processes. By recognising and addressing their own biases, researchers can conduct their work with integrity, ensuring that their findings are both reliable and ethically sound. This self-awareness is vital to maintain the quality and impact of research, guiding researchers to navigate their work conscientiously and with full accountability.

The power of words, subjectivity and reflexivity

Research, like all social interactions, is laden with power dynamics that must be carefully navigated. If you are a researcher affiliated with an academic institution, you inherently possess a degree of power. Additionally, factors like your economic status, gender, race and age can confer further influence. In contexts such as Africa, it is crucial to confront and rethink the colonial legacies of research methods and to challenge their Euro-Western gaze.

Reflexivity

Reflexivity involves a critical reflection on how researchers construct knowledge. This reflective process encompasses all stages of research from planning and conducting a study to writing up findings. It demands awareness of the various influences that shape one's construction of knowledge and how these are manifested throughout the research process (Guillemin and Gillam, 2004). As a reflexive researcher, you must be able to critically evaluate your role and influence within the research setting, ensuring that personal biases and the research environment do not unduly skew the research outcomes.

The concept of objectivity in research, especially within the human sciences and creative arts, is contentious. Objectivity implies a lack of bias and a universal truth standard, but given the subjective nature of human experience and interpretation, achieving true neutrality is problematic. In *Whose Science? Whose Knowledge? Thinking from Women's Lives*, Sandra Harding (1991) argues that objectivity is intertwined with the researcher's perspective, shaped by their cultural, social and historical contexts. This suggests that in human sciences, objectivity might be an unrealistic goal, as research is fundamentally influenced by human factors.

The creative arts, including poetic inquiry, are increasingly recognised for their value in human sciences research. These fields often leverage subjectivity as a strength, providing deep insights into human experiences by engaging with the subjective and emotive aspects of understanding (Leavy, 2015).

While absolute objectivity may be elusive, achieving rigour and trustworthiness in research is crucial. Techniques such as prolonged engagement, member checking and methodical documentation enhance credibility. Your research might extend over a longer period, involve multiple interactions with participants or use follow-up focus groups to ensure that the findings authentically represent participant intentions (Lahman et al, 2010; Sliep, 2024).

Embracing the subjective nature of human experiences and artistic expression can enrich research outcomes, offering more complex and nuanced understandings. By adhering to rigorous standards, researchers can produce work that is both insightful and credible, effectively capturing the complexity of human conditions. There is a distinction between trustworthiness and rigour in poetic inquiry:

- **Trustworthiness** hinges on the authenticity of the voice being represented in research. It requires poems to accurately reflect the experiences, emotions and perspectives of participants, ensuring a balance between artistic expression and fidelity to original data. Techniques like member checking, where participants verify the accuracy of the poetic renditions of their narratives, are essential. Employing multiple data sources, methods or investigators can also enhance trustworthiness.
- **Rigour** demands clear and transparent documentation of the research process, including how data were collected, analysed and transformed into poetry. It involves adopting a stance of reflective practice where researchers critically examine their own biases and assumptions to maintain the integrity of the inquiry. This ensures that the research remains grounded in the data and adheres to methodological standards.

By integrating these principles, researchers can navigate the ethical and methodological complexities associated with poetic inquiry, fostering a research environment that respects participant voices and contributes meaningfully to social justice and change.

Inclusive representation

Increasingly, there is a call to move from Eurocentric methodologies towards encouraging scholars to embrace and value knowledge systems that colonialism has historically marginalised or silenced, even if some see it as epistemic disobedience and border thinking (Mignolo, 2011). Building on these ideas, feminist scholars such as Kimberlé Crenshaw (2017), Patricia Hill Collins (2019), bell hooks (2000) and Gayatri Chakravorty Spivak (2012) have contributed significant insights on research ethics. Crenshaw (1989) introduces the concept of intersectionality, which she describes as 'an analytic sensibility, a way of thinking about identity and its relationship to power' (Crenshaw, 2017, p 1).

Intersectionality highlights how multiple forms of oppression – such as those based on race and gender – intersect, particularly affecting women of colour by compounding forms of exclusion and discrimination. This framework is especially relevant in poetic inquiry, as it helps researchers explore how intersecting identities shape the narratives and expressions within their poetry. Researchers might experience privilege in some areas, such as academic status, while simultaneously facing discrimination related to gender, race or other identities. Figure 4.2 illustrates this principle.

Patricia Hill Collins emphasises the importance of bringing marginalised voices to the forefront of discussions, stating

Figure 4.2: Intersectionality

'intersectionality as critical social theory brings people who are often left on the margins to the centre of analysis' (Collins, 2019, p 30). Similarly, bell hooks advocates for a broad application of feminist principles: 'To be "feminist" in any authentic sense of the term is to want for all people, female and male, liberation from sexist role patterns, domination, and oppression' (hooks, 2000, p 26). This approach in research ethics promotes a diligent effort in poetic inquiry to question and break down typical power structures that poetry might reflect. This involves acknowledging our complex identities, recognising our positions of power or privilege and understanding the intersections of identities related to the themes we are exploring, with the aim of challenging racism.

Gayatri Chakravorty Spivak (2012) challenges researchers to listen to and amplify voices that are frequently ignored or silenced, particularly in postcolonial settings. Researchers are urged to deconstruct the matrix of social categories and hierarchical structures that perpetuate oppression, such as heteronormativity alongside racism, which may pose increased risks for Black lesbian women in certain environments. An in-depth understanding of the contextual histories, politics and cultural factors is essential and must be woven into the research respectfully (Smith, 2012).

We provide two exercises aimed at helping you to enhance reflexivity and understand power dynamics within your research. The first exercise is based on Yvonne's reflections and a poem about power dynamics in research.

> I am a White woman, which means I have benefited from the apartheid system in South Africa. I am married to a woman and have White and Black children, but that does not make me less privileged. I am a lecturer with a title and work with students, and in that context I carry a lot of power even if I train and teach in a Freirean way. Before I do research or teach, I need to check in – what power is present and how is this power operating? After I have taught or done a part of the research, I have to check again. I have to keep the dialogue open for others to alert me if I have blind spots. I need to breathe through the discomfort. Students call

me by my first name and my door is open for walk-ins. Where appropriate, I name power and privilege. I build in anonymous ways of giving feedback. I use peers to give me feedback. If data is collected, I will ask someone who is more representative of the group to do the interviews or focus group discussions, preferably in their mother tongue. We often involve creative ways of accessing knowledge where it is not the creativity that is evaluated but the self-reflected responses. For all of us, it stays a lifelong process.

'Less of me'

the seductive play of power
say this not that
highlight here not there
track and trace my power play
blow the whistle on my blind spots
breathe through the discomfort
until a closer truth is revealed
with less of me and more of you
in words and rhythm on paper

Exercise: positionality

1. Exploring positionality and power in research

This exercise will help you reflect on your positionality and the power dynamics at play in your research setting, thus improving the integrity and ethical grounding of your research practices.

1.1 Begin by reading Yvonne's reflections on her own positionality and the associated power dynamics. Notice how she identifies her privileges and the steps she takes to manage power responsibly.

1.2 Similar to Yvonne, write a short reflective essay about your own positionality. Consider your social, economic, educational and cultural background. Reflect on the privileges and powers these attributes may confer within your research context.

1.3 Address the following points in your reflection:
- How does your background benefit or hinder your research?
- What power dynamics arise from your position as a researcher?
- How do you plan to manage these dynamics ethically?
- What steps can you take to ensure inclusivity and fairness in your interactions with research participants?

1.4 Inspired by Yvonne's poem, 'Less of me', craft your own poem that explores the themes of power, positionality and reflexivity.

2. Exploring biases

- Identify and acknowledge biases that could affect your research.
- Reflect on potential preconceptions related to your research topic or participants. Document these biases and consider strategies to remain mindful of them throughout your research.
- Raise awareness of subjective influences on your research and promote rigorous, unbiased inquiry.

3. Writing poetry

- Use poetry to reflect on your positionality and biases.
- Craft a poem that captures your reflections on how your identity intersects with your research work, emphasising themes of self-awareness and reflexivity.

- Poetry serves as a creative outlet to express and explore the complexities of your identity and its impact on your research.

4. Developing reflexive practices

- Establish ongoing practices to maintain reflexivity in your research.
- Plan regular activities, such as maintaining a reflexive journal or engaging in peer discussions, to continually assess and reflect on your influence as a researcher.
- Ensure sustained self-awareness and ethical rigour in your research process.

5. Sharing and feedback (optional)

- Gain external perspectives on your reflexive practices.
- Share your positionality statement or reflexive poem with a colleague or mentor, and discuss your insights.
- Feedback can help illuminate blind spots in your self-reflection and enhance the depth of your reflexivity.

Exercise: exploring power and privilege through poetic inquiry

This exercise is designed to help you explore and articulate your thoughts on personal power and privilege, and how these influence your perspectives and interactions.

Step 1: Mapping power and privilege

- Take a piece of paper and create two columns labelled 'power' and 'privilege'.

- In the power column, note down the ways in which you wield power in different contexts (for example, think about the effect of your job role, age, gender, race or educational achievements).
- In the privilege column, list aspects of your identity or life circumstances that grant you privileges (for example, being able-bodied, having financial stability, being a member of a majority ethnic group).
- Consider how these elements of power and privilege intersect, such as the influence of an academic position in a scholarly setting.

Step 2: Composing a poem

- Using your reflections as inspiration, write a short poem that captures your feelings, realisations or questions about your own power and privilege. The format of the poem is flexible so let your creativity flow.
- If possible, share your poem in a discussion with a colleague or friend. Reflect on how the poem uncovers different layers of understanding about power and privilege. Consider the implications of juxtaposing privilege with responsibilities and the overall purpose of your research.

Step 3: Doing deeper analysis

- Look for common themes, unexpected insights and the emotional resonances within the poems.
- Assess how using poetry has deepened your understanding of power and privilege.
- Critical questions:
  - What types of power relations are present in your research setting?

- How does your research or poetry make these power dynamics visible?
- How do research participants handle power dynamics?
- What additional measures can you implement to disrupt and address harmful power dynamics?

We hope these exercises have deepened your understanding of your own positionality and how it enhances your ability to conduct ethically responsible and informed research. It is important to recognise that managing power dynamics and practicing reflexivity are continuous processes. Regular self-evaluation and adaptation of your methods are essential to ensure they remain ethically sound.

Poetic inquiry as a catalyst for social change

Poetic inquirers worldwide, including scholars such as Faulkner (2007) and Prendergast (2009), highlight the crucial role of creative arts in amplifying marginalised voices and challenging entrenched colonial narratives. Poetic inquiry seeks not only to empower these groups but also to provoke reflection and transformation within privileged circles (Stein and Mankowski, 2004). This reflective process acts as a societal mirror, revealing inequities and biases and encouraging critical introspection among those in positions of power.

The intersection of poetic inquiry and social change is notable for its capacity to merge artistic expression with critical social analysis. By incorporating an awareness of power dynamics into our poems, we give voice to societal inequalities, fostering social commentary and potential reform.

Poetic inquiry uniquely challenges conventional narratives and introduces new ways of understanding. Through the use of metaphors, rhythm and other poetic devices, it articulates complex social issues in ways that question dominant discourses and suggest alternative perspectives. This disruption is vital for social change, as it opens new avenues for thought and action.

The box on the social justice goals of poetic inquiry highlights how the participatory nature of poetic inquiry is decolonial and can serve social justice.

The participatory nature and social justice goals of poetic inquiry

Much of poetic inquiry is inherently participatory, aligning well with the aims of social justice research, which include:

- **Equity and equality:** Focus on identifying and addressing the roots of inequity in areas such as education, healthcare and housing. How can research uncover disparities in access and outcomes across different groups?
- **Human rights and dignity:** Investigate issues related to human rights abuses and the exploitation of vulnerable populations.
- **Empowerment and agency:** Explore ways to empower marginalised groups and enhance their self-advocacy, using methods like found poetry to emphasise participants' own words.
- **Inclusive policy writing:** Use research outcomes to inform policy making that addresses social injustices and supports equitable practices.
- **Intersectionality:** Examine how overlapping forms of discrimination impact individuals uniquely, affecting their experiences of oppression and privilege.
- **Systemic analysis:** Study the structural causes of social injustices, including institutional practices and legal frameworks.
- **Community engagement:** Employ participatory research methods that involve community members directly affected by social injustices, ensuring their active participation in the research process.
- **Advocacy and activism:** Link research with advocacy efforts aimed at social change.
- **Global and local perspectives:** Address social justice from both global and local viewpoints, acknowledging the global interconnections and the significance of local specifics.
- **Multidisciplinary approaches:** Use theories and methodologies from various fields to tackle complex social justice challenges comprehensively (Figure 4.3 illustrates this).

Democratising research through community involvement

By involving community members, especially those from marginalised backgrounds, in both the creation and interpretation

Figure 4.3: Multidisciplinarity

of poetic works, the research process becomes more democratic and inclusive. This approach both enhances the research and ensures it faithfully represents the lived experiences of its subjects. Ideally, such collaborative research can catalyse social change.

Heidi van Rooyen and her team (2021) exemplified this approach by engaging with trans women in Namibia to co-create a series of 10 found poems. This collaborative effort not only highlighted the participants' experiences but also positioned the research to potentially influence societal perceptions and policies.

'Nobody is safe'

You find these boys,
they target you.
Alone or in a group,
they pick you out.

Nobody is safe.
Especially trans women.

They wait for you.
You walk home,
they rob you.
If you don't have anything,
they hit you
humiliate you.

When they rob cis women,
they don't rape her
or sexually assault her.
They always rape trans women.
They think you were born a man
but behave like a woman.
Today, they'll show you.

Social spaces aren't safe.
Out having your fun,
drinking your beer –
a dude just comes
and kicks you for no reason.
You did nothing.

You fall to the ground.
Nobody, nobody, nobody,
will help you.

The crowd mocks
adds fuel to the fire
stands and stares
'till the guy is done.

The engagement with the series of found poems was a profound, embodied experience for the trans women involved, providing them with a powerful means of expressing their realities. For the researchers, this activity offered a deeper, more empathetic understanding of the discrimination and challenges faced by the participants. Such poetic collaborations help bridge the gap between academic inquiry and lived experience, enriching the research with authentic insights and fostering a closer connection between researchers and the communities they study.

> ### Exercise: decolonising research through poetic inquiry
>
> This exercise will help you reflect on how you can engage in a decolonial way within your research.
>
> 1. Choose a poem you have written during your research. This poem should ideally relate to the themes you are exploring in your work.
> 2. Use the poem as a basis for a deep reflective exercise. Consider the following questions, informed by Ohito and Nyachee (2018, in Faulkner, 2019), to guide your analysis:
>   - Whose voices are present in the poem, and whose are absent? Are you amplifying marginalised voices or reinforcing dominant narratives?
>   - Does your voice in the poem challenge prevailing discourses about identity? How does it do this?
>   - What does your poem reveal about your own identity and its intersection with the research topic?
>   - What potential for social action does your poem suggest? How might it contribute to social change?
>   - How can practices of co-generating knowledge be implemented or improved in your research?
>   - How can your poetic inquiry problematise or contribute to discussions on justice and transformation?
> 3. Write down your responses to these questions. This will help you critically engage with your own research practices and enhance the decolonial lens through which you view your work.

Using a pantoum structure to include diverse voices

Using a pantoum structure to include diverse voices is highly effective in the context of poetic inquiry. Introduced in Chapter 2, the pantoum's primary strength lies in its repetitive pattern which emphasises and re-examines key ideas or emotions by revisiting them in successive stanzas. This iterative process is invaluable in research, where re-evaluating concepts or experiences deeply enhances understanding.

The pantoum's repetitive nature not only fosters contemplation but also intensifies the emotional depth of human experiences, which is central to poetic inquiry. It mirrors the recursive nature of memory and thought, reflecting how individuals often process their experiences and emotions. This makes the pantoum particularly potent for exploring complex, multifaceted topics common in qualitative research.

Despite its structured format, the pantoum allows significant creative freedom. The fixed repetition of lines ensures continuity and coherence, while the introduction of new elements in alternating lines allows for dynamic thematic exploration. This combination of repetition and novelty provides a balanced approach to engaging with human experience, making the pantoum a versatile and effective tool in poetic inquiry.

Example of a pantoum

Here is an example of a pantoum crafted by Yvonne Sliep et al (2022), derived from phrases contributed by students and facilitators engaged in a process to become more reflexive in their professional lives.

> 'walking the talk is a lifelong process'
>
> *prepare to learn, relearn and unlearn*
> *to stand even if standing is uncomfortable*
> *unpack my blind spots, see the privileges I did not earn*
> *what do I do, when am I culpable?*
>
> *to stand even if standing is uncomfortable*
> *breathing through the discomfort*
> *what do I do, when am I culpable?*
> *our accountability must become overt*

breathing through the discomfort
being intentional about our voices and actions
our accountability must become overt
some will follow in the footsteps of those that went ahead

being intentional about our voices and actions
I'm navigating how to be true to myself
some will follow in the footsteps of those that went ahead
walking the talk is a lifelong process

I'm navigating how to be true to myself
unpack my blind spots, see the privileges I did not earn
walking the talk is a lifelong process
prepare to learn, relearn, and unlearn

Exercise: pantoum for multiple voices

Initial reflection: Consider the concept of diversity within the scope of your research. Identify voices that are typically marginalised or overlooked. Reflect on how their perspectives could enrich the understanding of your study's themes.

Writing the pantoum:

1. Select 12 impactful lines or sentences from your research interviews.

2. Write each line on a separate piece of paper.

3. Arrange these in front of you in a random sequence.

4. Construct a 12-line pantoum using the guidelines in Chapter 2. This involves repeating specific lines in a set pattern, which helps to emphasise the cyclical nature of themes and perspectives.

Reflecting on the poem: After you have written your pantoum, spend some time contemplating what this poetic form reveals about the integration of diverse voices in your

> research. Consider how the repetitive structure of the pantoum might mirror the recurring significance of these perspectives in understanding the broader context of your study. Reflect on any new insights gained and evaluate how they might affect the direction or conclusions of your research.

Understanding yourself as a reflexive poetic inquirer

As we delve further into reflexivity, it is crucial to cultivate a deep understanding of yourself as a poetic inquirer. This skill is honed through persistent practice, encompassing continual self-awareness and critical examination of how your role as a researcher influences both the research environment and your interactions with participants.

Reflexivity involves recognising and addressing the biases and preconceptions you bring into the research process. This is particularly significant given that many researchers have been educated within colonial systems that often marginalise indigenous languages and ways of knowing. These systems not only appropriated land and disrupted lives but also sought to erase diverse epistemologies and ontologies (Bhattacharya, 2020).

Developing reflexivity means actively questioning how these influences shape your research practices and striving to integrate more inclusive and culturally sensitive methodologies. It requires being mindful of the power dynamics at play and making conscious efforts to understand and incorporate the perspectives of those who have been historically under-represented or misunderstood.

In the rest of this section, we offer a collection of poems paired with reflective exercises designed to refine your skills and practice as a reflexive researcher-poet or poet-researcher.

Exploring liminal spaces through poetic inquiry

In poetic inquiry, writing about liminal spaces invites us into a realm of profound exploration and potential transformation. Gloria Anzaldúa (1987) highlights the depth and richness of this journey, emphasising how poetry allows us to venture into areas of ourselves and our experiences that remain uncharted, even to us. Liminal spaces, those transitional zones between known and unknown, being and becoming, offer fertile ground for poetic exploration. They are places of ambiguity, complexity, contradiction and flux, where fixed boundaries dissolve and the conventional structures we rely on are upended.

Engaging with liminal spaces in poetic inquiry pushes us beyond the comfort of certainty into a realm brimming with possibilities. Here, in the ambivalence and fluidity of these in-between zones, new understandings and identities can emerge. This process is not about seeking immediate answers or clarity but rather embracing the uncertainty and the transformative potential it holds.

Writing into liminality allows us to question, to wonder and to imagine. It invites us to consider the experiences of marginalisation or the process of embracing non-dominant identities with openness and curiosity. Such exploration can lead to ground-breaking insights and expressions, offering a glimpse into the complex, often overlooked aspects of human experience.

The following is an example of writing about the experience of embracing non-dominant identities:

'Belonging begins in exile'

She enters the tall-ceilinged building
The hairstyles and dress code
All slightly off the straight bent
Of the primary school soccer mom's
I'd become accustomed to
'They' in this case a pronoun of inclusion
rather than exclusion
Will they smell childbirth on her skin
Will they detect the marks of motherhood
Will they reject her un-queer hair

Surrounded by people who have 'come out',
Who have stood up to the norm
Who dared to find their own voice
Can she find belonging, after conforming for so long?

Her lover slips her hand under her ribcage
And for that delicious moment she belongs

In incorporating her observations about identity into her research topic, Hough exemplifies how poetic inquiry can be a powerful tool for exploring complex social issues. The poem reflects the liminal experiences of identity: those in-between states where individuals may feel neither fully included nor completely ostracised. By articulating these nuances, the poem encourages a deeper examination of what it means to belong and how individuals navigate the boundaries of their identities in different contexts.

Exercise: discovering yourself as a reflexive poetic inquirer

This exercise aims to deepen your understanding of yourself as a poetic inquirer and enhance your reflexivity by exploring the lived realities of research participants through the lens of your own cultural background.

1. Choose a language

- If English is not your first language, you are encouraged to write this exercise in your preferred language. This approach allows you to express thoughts and emotions more fluidly and capture the nuances of your cultural metaphors.

2. Free writing

- Begin by reflecting on the experiences and stories shared by your research participants. What aspects of their lives strike you the most? What moves you about their realities?
- Write freely for 10–15 minutes. Let your thoughts flow without worrying about structure or correctness. The goal is to capture raw emotions and the reflections that arise.

3. Incorporate cultural metaphors

- Integrate metaphors and expressions from your own cultural background that resonate with the themes or experiences you are writing about. This inclusion enriches the text by embedding deeper cultural significances and perspectives.

4. Translate and reflect

- If you have written in a language other than English, translate your poem into English. This step is essential if you plan to include this poem in an English-language academic write-up.

- Reflect on the translation process: how does the poem change when it shifts between languages? What nuances are lost or gained?

5. Read the inspiration poem

- Read the inspiration poem 'The light', which follows this exercise. It is written by an author who delves into her identity and the impact of her experiences. Notice how her cultural and personal insights shape the poem's message and form.

- Let this poem inspire your writing. How does the author embody her identity? How can you use her approach to tap into your own experiences and cultural understanding?

6. Share and discuss

- If possible, share your poem with a peer or a group. Discuss the different cultural elements each of you has brought into your poems. What have you learned about each other's perspectives and experiences?

> • Discuss how this exercise has affected your understanding of reflexivity and your role as a poetic inquirer. How can these insights influence your future research practices?

'The light'

I am rediscovering my language
My tongue learns to uncoil the serpent of ancestry
As my mouth wraps around the words of
my forefathers in
Salutation to the sun
I am drinking wine from the vines that sprout from
my veins
Intoxicated by my own being
Drunk on my true identity as a spirit here, as a queen,
as a god
I breathe underwater now
Having reintroduced myself to the sea and the rivers
I swim with mermaid magic rippling off my tale as
I reawaken the
fairy tale in this living, wave after wave
My hips spark flames when my body sways around
fire chanting
anthems to the full moon
The mystery of creation
I am the woman who makes gods swoon
The seductress of incarnation conjuring life in my womb
I am shielded by the flesh of millions
I wear my mother's skin in blizzards
I am she who was fetishised, exhibitionised, demolished and
the crucified.
Here to rise again and ascend into the glory of my
divine feminine.
I am the chorus at dawn
The voice of my ancestors reborn
As they take the form of all the rich yesterdays in
my tomorrow

All the golden joy in my sorrow
All the royalty in my blood
All the mortality in my bones
I do not walk alone
I run with the wind who knows my true names
I fly with the eagle who sees my real greatness
I slither with snakes who remind me to stay grounded
I flourish like the glory with which I was fearfully made

The last exercise is designed not only to cultivate your skills in poetic inquiry but also to enhance your sensitivity to the diverse cultural contexts of the participants you study. It encourages a thoughtful examination of how personal and cultural identities intersect with research narratives, promoting a more inclusive and reflexive approach to research.

Example: identity and positionality

In the following example, a student, Sipho Ngcongo, shares his life story in a co-created poem with Yvonne Sliep, who witnessed his story and offered back what she heard (the poem appears in Sliep et al, 2021). This poem provides a textured description of the challenging background from which the student comes:

'Bad blood'

lots of bodies moving around chaotically
bad blood amongst all of us
and nowhere at all to go to
violence sparks grudges and jealousy
and nowhere at all to go to

first my father was stabbed
six times in the chest
the day six cows were slaughtered
to change the wrath
of the ancestors

then my brother was stabbed
five times in the back
all in the name of envy
punished because he dared
to go to varsity

I know
I am next in line
I know
it is coming
I too go to varsity

I do not know
who I am
I do not know
where I want to go to
I know it has to be away from here

Later in the process, Ngcongo writes a poem that speaks about the empowering impact of engaging in dialogue in a safe space (this appears in Sliep et al, 2021):

'Re-authoring'

I found strength in dialogue
speaking of and not into my circumstances
I develop skills to navigate a complex and diverse terrain
Confidently and flexible I take on challenges
knowing we don't know all the answers
I reclaimed my space and became visible
from airborne roots and broken branches
to power kindling from within
I no longer dream about agency
I have self-efficacy and will generate more

so here I am
I bring my truest self with me
re-authoring my identity

> *doing hope in an unknown landscape*
> *with positive uncertainty*

These poems are used in a chapter that challenges positionality in the academic environment. Instead of only referring to Ngcongo's life story, he is recognised as a co-author in the chapter, reflecting a shift towards more equitable and inclusive academic practices (Sliep et al, 2021).

The box on reflective inquiry questions pulls together some key prompts that you can refer to as you move forwards and embark on a journey of being an ethical, reflexive and powerful poetic inquirer who does research that is transformative in your contexts and for the participants you work alongside.

Reflective poetic inquiry questions

We continually grapple with showing how we contribute to science through poetic inquiry (Vincent, 2018). Here are some reflective questions drawn from personal poetic inquiry experiences – these may be used to guide your reflective practice (Sliep, 2024).

- How does my relationship to the people or events that I am researching affect my perspective?
- What assumptions or biases do I bring to my observations, and how might these shape the way I interpret and represent the data?
- How can I ensure that my research is not exploitative or harmful?
- How can I use the insights gained through poetic inquiry to create positive change and social transformation, rather than simply observing or documenting experiences?
- Have I obtained informed consent from the individuals and communities involved in these stories, and are they aware of the purpose and potential impact of sharing their experiences?
- Have I taken adequate steps to protect the anonymity and privacy of the individuals and communities involved, and have I considered the potential consequences of disclosing their identities or specific details?
- Am I presenting these stories with respect and dignity, acknowledging the resilience, strength and agency of individuals and communities rather than perpetuating stereotypes or reinforcing victimhood?

- Have I adequately acknowledged and respected the cultural and social context of the individuals and communities in these stories, and have I made efforts to understand and represent their perspectives and experiences accurately and authentically? Do I recognise my own cultural lens?
- Where possible, am I engaging in ongoing dialogue and collaboration with the individuals and communities involved in these stories, to ensure that their voices are heard and respected throughout the research process?
- Have I reflected on my own positionality, biases and potential blind spots as a researcher, and how these might affect my interpretation and presentation of these stories?

These questions encourage a deep and critical engagement with the ethical dimensions of poetic inquiry, ensuring that the research is conducted with integrity and respect for all participants involved.

'How does it sit?'

Is it logical?
come with ease?
Or is it a pest?
like mice or mites?
Ants in your pants
that itch and bite?
Or a post-mortem
to reflect the past?

Is it silly?
a messy mix
of apples plus figs
of geese plus pigs
of pears plus peas
of flies in trees
or even poison ivy?

Is it stoical?
a pope in prayer

show remorse
be aware
mope or pore
raise or praise
as you may

Is it misty?
a soft spray
a palm at sea
a flimsy foam
of salty tears
roaming loops
at times aloof

To me
it is at times
gigantic, magic
a tantalising tease
to excite
to release
orgasmic,
I become alive
as I flex
my optic view

Craft a map
prepare to stray
Immerse myself
in your, in my
life stories
Lost, stop
Found, stop
Start all over
Reflexively

Reflective note on poetry writing in research

As you engage in poetic inquiry, it is important to remember that not every poem needs to serve a formal purpose in your research manuscript. Poetry, in this context, is also a valuable tool for developing your reflexivity and honing your skills as a poet.

Here are a few key points to keep in mind:

1. **Practice makes perfect:** Regular writing exercises can improve your ability to express complex thoughts and emotions succinctly and poignantly. Consider your poetry writing as practice in the craft.
2. **Poetry can be a tool for reflexivity:** Writing poetry allows you to explore and articulate your thoughts and feelings about the research process and your subject matter in a nuanced way. This can help you understand your biases and perspectives more deeply.
3. **There can be flexibility in expression:** Not every piece needs to tackle serious or heavy themes. Poetry can also be a space for lightness, exploring a range of emotions and experiences that inform your scholarly work.
4. **Poetry can be used for personal development:** Use poetry to explore personal insights or to challenge your own thinking. This not only aids your personal growth but also enhances your capabilities as a researcher.
5. **There is no pressure for perfection:** The poems you write do not all have to be candidates for publication. Some can simply serve as reflective practice or methodological experiments.

By integrating poetry writing into your routine, not only as a research method but also as a personal and professional development tool, you ensure that your work remains vibrant, thoughtful and deeply human.

Conclusion

Adopting a decolonising ethical approach to poetic inquiry involves a deep understanding of power dynamics, recognition of colonial legacies, incorporation of feminist and intersectional methodologies, and a critical examination of how indigenous knowledge is acknowledged or dismissed. By engaging ethically, you heighten awareness of the potential emotional impacts of your work and ensure that you revisit your poetic outputs with research participants to verify authenticity and minimise harm, thereby striving for beneficence. This process includes raising awareness among your audience and advocating for social action.

It is essential to maintain openness, constructiveness and cooperation when negotiating ethical practices with research participants and other interested people (Hopkins, 2015). Poetic inquiry calls for creating alternative spaces and new ways of understanding that move beyond colonial frameworks. This not only changes how research is conducted but also how knowledge is perceived and valued.

By integrating these diverse perspectives, poetic inquiry can serve as a potent tool for social change, giving a platform to voices typically marginalised and providing insights that challenge and deepen our global understanding. In this transformative process, you play a crucial role in effecting change.

References

Alcott, L. (1988) 'Cultural feminism versus post-structuralism: the identity crisis in feminist theory', *Signs*, 13(3): 405–36.

Anzaldúa, G.E. (1987) *Borderlands/La Frontera: The New Mestiza*, San Francisco: Aunt Lute Books.

Bhattacharya, K. (2020) 'Cultivating resonant images through poetic meditation: a de/colonial approach to educational research', in E. Fitzpatrick and K. Fitzpatrick (eds) *Poetry, Method, and Education Research*, New York: Routledge, pp 155–71.

Chilisa, B. (2012) *Indigenous Research Methodologies*, Thousand Oaks, CA: Sage Publications.

Collins, P.H. (2019) *Intersectionality as Critical Social Theory*, Durham, NC: Duke University Press.

Crenshaw, K. (1989) 'Demarginalizing the intersection of race and sex: a Black feminist critique of antidiscrimination doctrine, feminist theory and antiracist politics', *University of Chicago Legal Forum*, 1: art 8, 139–67.

Crenshaw, K. (2017) *On Intersectionality: Essential Writings*, New York: The New Press.

Faulkner, S.L. (2007) *Poetry as Method: Reporting Research through Verse*, Walnut Creek, CA: Left Coast Press.

Faulkner, S.L. (2019) *Poetic Inquiry: Craft, Method, and Practice*, London: Routledge.

Guillemin, M. and Gillam, L. (2004) 'Ethics, reflexivity, and "ethically important moments" in research', *Qualitative Inquiry*, 10(2): 261–80.

Harding, S. (1991) *Whose Science? Whose Knowledge? Thinking from Women's Lives*, Ithaca, NY: Cornell University Press.

Harris, I. (2023) 'The light', in H. van Rooyen (ed) *Voices Unbound: Poems of the Eighth International Symposium on Poetic Inquiry*, Cape Town: Africa Sun Press, pp 99–100.

hooks, b. (2000) *Feminism Is for Everybody: Passionate Politics*, Cambridge, MA: South End Press.

Hopkins, P.E. (2015) 'Positionalities and knowledge: negotiating ethics in practice', *ACME: An International Journal for Critical Geographies*, 6(3): 386–94.

Lahman, M.K., Geist, M.R., Rodriguez, K.L., Graglia, P.E., Richard, V.M. and Schendel, R.K. (2010) 'Poking around poetically: research, poetry, and trustworthiness', *Qualitative Inquiry*, 16(1): 39–48.

Leavy, P. (2015) *Method Meets Art: Arts-Based Research Practice*, New York: Guilford Press.

Mignolo, W. (2011) *The Darker Side of Western Modernity: Global Futures, Decolonial Options*, Durham, NC: Duke University Press.

Ndlovu, D.S. (2022) 'Own my life today', *Health Promotion Practice*, 23(6): 924.

Orb, A., Eisenhauer, L. and Wynaden, D. (2001) 'Ethics in qualitative research', *Journal of Nursing Scholarship*, 33(1): 93–6.

Pedri-Spade, C. (2016) ' "The drum is your document" decolonizing research through Anishinabe song and story', *International Review of Qualitative Research*, 9(4): 385–406.

Prendergast, M., Leggo, C. and Sameshima, P. (eds) (2009) *Poetic Inquiry: Vibrant Voices in the Social Sciences*, Rotterdam: Sense Publishers.

Sliep, Y. (2012) 'We compose our own requiem: an autoethnographic study of mourning', *Creative Approaches to Research* (special issue: Poetic inquiry: seeing, caring, understanding), 5(2): 6–85.

Sliep, Y. (2024) 'Witnessing across hemisphere through Haibun: vox spectare', in A. Vincent (ed) *Poetic Inquiry Atlas Vol 1: A Survey of Rigorous Poetics*, Wilmington, DE: Vernon Press, pp 199–212.

Sliep, Y., Makhakhe, N., Ngcongo, S. and Calmes, B. (2021) 'Working with life stories for transformational learning', in C. Kagan, R. Lawthom, A.X.Z. Zambrano, J.A.A. Inzunza, M. Richards and J. Akhurst (eds) *The Routledge International Handbook of Community Psychology: Facing Global Crises with Hope*, Oxford: Routledge, pp 355–70.

Smith, L.T. (2012) *Decolonizing Methodologies* (2nd edn), London: Zed Books.

Spivak, G.C. (2012) *An Aesthetic Education in the Era of Globalization*, Cambridge, MA: Harvard University Press.

Stein, C.H. and Mankowski, E.S. (2004) 'Asking, witnessing, interpreting, knowing: conducting qualitative research in community psychology', *American Journal of Community Psychology*, 33: 21–35.

van Rooyen, H., Essack, Z., Mahali, A., Groenewald, C. and Solomons, A. (2021) '"The power of the poem": using poetic inquiry to explore trans-identities in Namibia', *Arts and Health*, 13(3): 315–28.

Vincent, A. (2018) 'Is there a definition? Ruminating on poetic inquiry, strawberries, and the continued growth of the field', *Art/Research International: A Transdisciplinary Journal*, 3(2): 48–76.

5

Assessing the craft and reach of poetic inquiry

Duduzile S. Ndlovu and Heidi van Rooyen

> This chapter addresses the dual perspectives of assessing the quality of poetic inquiry while considering its broader implications for audience engagement. It is rooted in principles from qualitative and arts-based research, emphasising the need for rigorous and aesthetic evaluations that meet both scientific and artistic standards. It is important to take the decolonial approach to poetic inquiry, which seeks to include marginalised voices and ensure that research outputs are accessible and meaningful across diverse communities.

Introduction

As we delve into this chapter, we address two pivotal questions that you may have considered on your journey through the earlier chapters of this book. If these questions have not yet emerged for you, we hope this discussion will inspire reflection. The first question centres on the validity of our poetic inquiry: how do we ascertain that our poetic inquiry is sufficiently robust? Or, to put it differently, how do we evaluate the quality of our research poems? The second question probes the purpose and reach of our work: who is the intended audience for our research?

Evaluating the quality of poetic inquiry is crucial. Sandra Faulkner (2019, p 102) expresses her concerns with some academic poetry, noting:

> My interest in poetic craft was born out of frustration with some poetry published as academic research that seemed sloppy, ill-conceived, and unconsidered. Just because research poetry is published in academic journals, read at academic conferences, or merely labelled academic, does not mean we should not consider poetic craft, especially when poets spend considerable time studying craft issues in an effort to further their aesthetics.

This critique underscores the necessity of honouring poetic traditions and the legacy of poets who have functioned as beacons of truth in various communities by meticulously engaging with the craft of poetry.

Johan Higgs (2008) asserts that creative representations of research can be subpar and suggests that researchers should undergo formal training in any artistic discipline they wish to employ to present their findings. Similarly, Knowles and Promislow (2008) argue that choosing art inquiry demands a significant commitment from the researcher, as it involves deep engagement with the artistic process.

In this book, we adopt a decolonial approach to poetic inquiry. Therefore, when assessing the quality of poetic inquiry, decoloniality serves as a foundational principle. This leads us to our second question about the audience for our research. In the Global South, research narratives about previously colonised populations often continue to reflect a colonial perspective. This makes it imperative to consider who our research engages and how it reaches audiences beyond our usual academic circles.

Next, we consider the quality and evaluation methods of poetic inquiry, and this is followed by a thorough exploration of the audience.

Quality of poetic inquiry

Consider this crucial question as we proceed: who benefits from, and who can access, the insights we generate through our poetic inquiry?

> **Exercise: can anyone write poetry for research?**
>
> Reflect on whether anyone can write poetry for research. Write a short paragraph of three to five sentences or set a timer and write for three minutes, expressing your thoughts on this topic. You can support a stance of yes, no or maybe. Save your response, as we will revisit it later in the chapter.

Assessing the quality of poetic inquiry

In evaluating poetic inquiry, we consider the expectations of both artistic and scientific communities. This dual focus raises critical questions: How can our outputs satisfy the criteria for high-quality art and rigorous science at the same time? What principles and values should underpin our work to qualify it as exemplary decolonial research? Faulkner's critique, referenced earlier, underscores the importance of honouring the craft of poetry while also meeting the standards of sound research. Andrew Sparkes (2020) discusses the role of non-poets or research-poets in poetic inquiry. He suggests that their poems can be viewed as not quite poetry, 'poemish' or good enough in that they still accomplish their representational task of using poetry to tell another's story (as illustrated in Figure 5.1). In these situations, you still bring science and art together, but allow space for the growth of the aspiring poetic inquirer over time.

Evaluating poetic inquiry in scientific method

Poetic inquiry involves creatively reconfiguring words to enhance our understanding of the world in complex ways. Poetic inquiry is a subset of arts-based research, which itself is a part of the broader qualitative research framework. To evaluate poetic inquiry

Figure 5.1: Poemish is good enough

effectively, it is crucial to understand the general principles of qualitative research, the specific nuances of arts-based research and how these principles apply to poetic inquiry. This comprehensive approach ensures that the evaluation of poetic inquiry respects both its artistic and its scientific foundations.

To evaluate poetic inquiry as research, it is essential to consider the frameworks of qualitative and arts-based research:

1. **Qualitative research framework:** Qualitative research is not concerned with generalising results or replicating studies, but emphasises the researcher's positionality and the interpretive nature of the findings. In qualitative research, traditional notions of validity are replaced with 'trustworthiness', which requires both rigour and relevance. Researchers are expected to demonstrate a systematic and meticulous approach, allowing for external evaluation of their methods (Finlay, 2006).
2. **Arts-based research considerations:** As part of arts-based research, poetic inquiry must meaningfully engage with artistic processes, ensuring that the creative representations significantly contribute to understanding the research phenomena.

There is a fine balance here, as illustrated in Figure 5.2. We turn next to how to tackle this issue of thoughtfully working with qualitative data and the broader concept of 'thinking qualitatively'.

What does it mean to think qualitatively?

To think qualitatively is to adopt a perspective that is deeply exploratory and inherently inquisitive, characterised by a sense of wonder, feelings of discomfort and a questioning attitude (Swaminathan and Mulvihill, 2018). This approach to research emphasises flexibility and adaptability, allowing researchers to modify their questions as new insights emerge. Additionally, qualitative thinking involves scrutinising data sources to construct coherent narratives or identify underlying themes. As researchers journey through this process of discovery, they dig into the depths of their data and synthesise it to build compelling narratives or identify themes. Importantly, the researcher is the instrument of measurement (Patton, 1990).

Figure 5.2: Evaluating poetic inquiry

Evaluating the quality of poetic inquiry thus starts with assessing whether the work embodies this comprehensive and reflexive qualitative thinking. Here are some guiding questions to help evaluate this aspect of your research.

Guiding questions to thinking qualitatively

1. Is the researcher able to see the patterns emerging from the data, some of which are unexpected or may contradict previous knowledge and experience?
2. Has the researcher interrogated how previous knowledge and experience may influence how they read and analyse the data. Are they able to 'hold' these while allowing the data to speak?
3. Has the researcher stayed true to the data generated in the research even where it goes against expectations?
4. What story is the researcher crafting and narrating out of the research?

While several of the preceding questions focus on the researcher's interpretation of data, feminist theorising underscores the importance of social location in shaping our perceptions of the world (Palmary, 2005). Throughout this book, we have encouraged critical reflection on how various social locations and positionalities affect the researcher's role in their research. This consideration becomes even more critical in decolonial poetic inquiry, where research is viewed as collaborative knowledge production between the researcher and participants. This collaborative approach allows for a nuanced examination of the power dynamics within research relationships. We revisit the idea of the researcher as an instrument later in this chapter, specifically in the context of poetic inquiry as a decolonial practice.

Barone and Eisner (2011) point out that arts-based research, including poetic inquiry, may not often achieve the status of a work of art. While striving for high artistic quality is important, the primary goal for researchers should not be to create the most exemplary piece of poetry. Instead, focus should be on the craft to ensure that the research representations are rigorously constructed and not careless. According to Leavy (2017), representation and audience should be considered from the start of the research. The chosen art form should effectively generate and convey the research content while engaging the intended audience – criteria Leavy refers to as the 'strength of the form'. She poses critical questions for evaluating arts-based research, such as: Does it tell a story? Is it coherent? Does it adhere to the norms of the chosen medium? And, crucially, does it use its aesthetic qualities to powerfully communicate the research findings?

Knowles and Promislow (2008) argue that the decision to use arts-based inquiry should be influenced by whether it aligns with the researcher's worldview, fits the research focus, matches the researcher's artistic skills, has potential for unique insights and can reach typically inaccessible audiences. These considerations underscore the importance of choosing an approach that not only enriches understanding but also broadens the impact of research through artistic expression.

When assessing the suitability of artistic forms for presenting research, it is crucial to choose the medium that best aligns with the research content and the researcher's capabilities. This consideration is vital for ensuring that the chosen art form can

Table 5.1: Criteria for evaluating arts-based research

Criteria	Questions to consider
Incisiveness	Does it cut to the core of an issue?
Conciseness	Does the art use the least space or fewest words to convey the message?
Coherence	Do the different parts come together well?
Generativity	Does the art cause the audience to view the world differently?
Social significance	Does the art make a difference in the world?
Evocation and illumination	What does the art make audiences feel and understand?

Source: Adapted from Barone and Eisner (2011)

adequately represent the research findings and effectively engage the intended audience. However, as previously mentioned, adopting a qualitative thinking approach also necessitates flexibility and responsiveness to the data as the research progresses.

The importance of initially selecting an appropriate art form cannot be overstated – it ensures that the researcher is adequately prepared, and that the artistic representation aligns with the research objectives from the start. Nonetheless, it is equally important to remain open to adjustments based on how the research unfolds. For instance, a researcher might start with the intention of creating a series of poems, but as the data is collected and analysed, it may become clear that the data is not suited to the poetic genre and perhaps a free form verse would better serve the data. Such flexibility allows the research to truly resonate with the data collected, enhancing both the impact and the authenticity of the final presentation. Table 5.1, based on insights from Barone and Eisner (2011), summarises the criteria for evaluating arts-based research.

Honing the craft of poetry

As Faulkner (2019) advocates, if your academic background did not include poetry but you are now considering using in your research, it is crucial to develop a solid understanding of poetic forms and techniques as discussed in Chapter 2.

Committing time to learn the craft of poetry is essential. There are several approaches to improving your poetic skills:

1. **Enrol in a poetry course:** There are many options, including online courses, workshops at local libraries or community centres, and university programmes. These structured learning environments can provide a comprehensive introduction to poetic forms and styles.
2. **Read widely:** Engage with a variety of poems from different genres and authors. This practice is not only enjoyable but also crucial for developing an ear for rhythm, language and the diverse ways poetry can convey meaning. It helps you to discover the types of poetry that resonate with you personally and informs your approach to incorporating poetry into your research.

By integrating these practices into your routine, you can significantly enhance your ability to use poetry as a powerful tool in academic research, bridging the gap between artistic expression and scientific inquiry.

Developing a poetic voice

Finding your poetic voice often begins by emulating poets whose work resonates with you. Spending time immersed in the works of admired poets can help you understand what styles and themes speak to you and sets a foundation for your own creative expression. Reading widely not only introduces you to various poetic forms and techniques but also inspires you to start crafting poems that reflect your unique perspective.

Practice is essential in mastering poetry. Regularly writing and revising your work sharpens your skills and deepens your understanding of poetry as a craft. Reading your poems aloud is a vital part of the revision process, helping you fine-tune rhythm, sound and expression. Experimenting with different poems from the same material can also reveal new insights and improve your versatility as a poet.

Participation in poetry writing groups offers community support and constructive feedback, crucial for growth and improvement.

Such groups provide a safe space to share your work and gain perspectives from fellow poetry enthusiasts.

Finding a mentor can be incredibly beneficial. A mentor who understands your artistic goals can offer tailored advice, constructive criticism and encouragement. However, it is important to choose the right environment for sharing your work. Sharing prematurely in unsupportive spaces can hinder confidence. Carefully select where and with whom you share your early drafts to protect and nurture your developing poetic voice.

It is a journey

The process of honing your poetry skills is like learning to drive: it requires practice, and true proficiency often comes only after formal qualification. Initially, your poetry might not meet your expectations but, with persistent practice, it can become 'good enough' to convey deeper insights into the complex experiences of others. This progression underscores the importance of recognising that each poem serves a unique purpose and should be evaluated based on its contextual relevance and the clarity of the process followed.

Patience and persistence are key. Like driving a vehicle, mastery over poetry does not occur overnight. It develops as you engage more frequently with the craft, each attempt bringing you closer to expressing ideas more effectively and evocatively. A poem that achieves a deeper understanding or conveys a unique perspective is valuable, even if it is not a masterpiece by conventional standards. This concept of 'good enough' poetry is crucial, especially when using poetry in research settings where the primary goal may be to illuminate rather than to dazzle.

When evaluating the quality of your poetic inquiry, consider Faulkner's criteria, which include artistic concentration, embodied experience, discovery or surprise, conditionality, narrative truth and transformation. Each of these elements can help guide your poetic endeavours, ensuring that your work not only meets academic and artistic standards but also resonates with authenticity and impact. Table 5.2, adapted from Faulkner's (2019) framework, provides a structured approach to assessing these aspects, encouraging a rigorous yet creative evaluation of poetic inquiry.

Table 5.2: Criteria for evaluating poetic inquiry

Criteria	Questions to consider
Artistic concentration	Are researchers studying the craft of poetry and paying attention to language (title, line breaks, words and so on)?
Embodied experience	Does the audience feel *with* the poem, not *about* the poem, and have an embodied experience of the truth of the poem from the metaphors used?
Discovery or surprise	Does the poem teach something familiar in a new way or change the way we see the mundane?
Conditionality	Is the point of view used to present the story through poetry?
Narrative truth	Is the poem based on a real event? (It may be imagined, but must ring true.)
Transformation	Does the poem provide new insight and give perspective? The audience must ask: Why am I receiving this information? What must I now do?

Source: Adapted from Faulkner (2019)

Exercise: evaluating poetic inquiry

This exercise is designed to deepen your understanding of the evaluation criteria for arts-based research and specifically for poetic inquiry. By comparing two different sets of evaluation criteria, you will develop a nuanced appreciation of what makes for effective poetic inquiry in research.

1. Read through Tables 5.1 and 5.2 – one on general arts-based research evaluation and the other specifically on poetic inquiry.

2. Reflect on the similarities and differences between the two sets of criteria. Consider how each set addresses the quality of the research and the artistic elements involved.

3. Write a short paragraph responding to one or more of the following prompts:
   - What similarities do you find between the two sets of criteria?
   - What differences stand out between them?

> - What are your thoughts on each of the criteria listed?
> - Highlight any words that stand out for you in your paragraph. Choose one word and use it as a prompt to write a short poem about evaluating your poetic inquiry.

The audience

In this section, we delve into a critical aspect of our research process: determining our audience. We begin this exploration by considering a pivotal question from Carl Leggo, a foundational figure in the field of poetic inquiry.

What is this poem good for?

Carl Leggo (2011) provocatively challenged researchers to consider 'What is this poem good for?' This question highlights the intrinsic value and purpose behind incorporating poetry into research. Poetry in research should be more than merely a trendy method; instead, its integration should focus on what it facilitates within the context of conveying research insights. Poetic inquiry should not be viewed as just another methodological tool applied mechanically to generate outcomes. Instead, poetry used in research can inject life into lived realities, which are often stripped away in the mechanistic ways in which we tend to report on peoples' lives in conventional academic research. According to Cutts (2020), writing poetry feels inherently right, serving as people's natural linguistic expression. Similarly, Williams (2023) describes poetry as a transformative space where people discover their voice and experience healing. This reflective perspective is essential to the impact and quality of poetic inquiry. We must consider not only the formal aspects of the research but also how it captures and communicates the essence of the inquiry, revitalising elements often lost in traditional academic research.

As we evaluate poetic inquiry, we also must consider its ability to reach beyond typical academic audiences, making research accessible and relevant to communities often excluded from scholarly discourse. This re-envisioning of the audience challenges and expands the impact of research, ensuring it contributes to broader societal understanding and inclusion.

Reflexive poems

Reflexive poetry within research serves not only as a methodological tool but also as a deeply personal practice that aids researchers in navigating the emotional complexities of their work. This type of poetry is often introspective, used by researchers to process personal and professional experiences encountered in the field. The evaluation of reflexive poems can differ significantly from the standard assessment of poetry for publication, since the primary audience is usually the researcher themselves – the poem may not be produced for an external audience.

1. **Evaluation of reflexive poetry:** Judging the quality of a reflexive poem might not hinge on its aesthetic qualities or adherence to poetic forms, but rather on its effectiveness in enhancing self-awareness and providing therapeutic value to the researcher. The key question here could be: how effectively does the poem help the researcher to process their experiences and emotions?
2. **Criteria for assessment:** A reflexive poem might focus on the impact of the research and the process of producing it on the researcher's wellbeing. For instance, the poem could help the researcher better understand their emotional and intellectual responses to subject matter or engagement with certain participants. It could contribute to a greater sense of resolution or peace for the researcher. This evaluative focus acknowledges the unique role of poetry in qualitative research as a tool for reflection and emotional processing.

For example, consider the reflexive poem 'This world' by Ndlovu (2020), which explores the complexities of conducting research during a personal and global crisis.

'This world'

A researcher
mother, black woman
My aunt has died.

I never met her, my father's cousin,
died in the time of covid19,
borders are closed.

Zimbabwean law says
burial has to happen within 48hrs.
Her daughter is in Botswana.

So, we WhatsApp
funeral sensibilities
acknowledging her passing

Virtual wake?
sharing scripture, hymns to comfort
we Ewallet[1] our financial tears.

I, researcher observing data?
The impact of covid19;
death.

Dare I write about
sacred mourning,
organise and archive this?

For who
to know and then,
do what?

This poem serves as a poignant example of how reflexive poetry can encapsulate the emotional and ethical dilemmas faced by researchers, offering insights into personal grief while questioning the implications of documenting such experiences.

The effectiveness of this poem could be measured by the clarity it brings to the researcher about their emotional landscape and the ethical considerations of their work.

Question to consider

As you progress through the section on audiences for research, keep the questions listed here in mind. When you complete the section, revisit these questions to consider how you might integrate what you have learned into your research practices.

1. How can we realistically expect non-academic audiences to engage with our research if it is presented in standard academic writing formats such as books or journal articles?
2. Do we aim for our research to be accessible only to a select few, or are we seeking broader, more meaningful engagement from a wider audience?
3. How can poetic inquiry expand the range of audiences that engage with and critique our work? What choices would you make in presenting your research to achieve this?
4. What motivations and goals underpin your use of poetic inquiry in research? How would you implement it?
5. Who participates in conceptualising the research project? What are the reasons for their involvement, and how is it facilitated?
6. How is participation in the project organised, and who determines the research focus?
7. What type of knowledge is emphasised in the research, and why?
8. Are alternative ways of knowing considered and respected within the research framework?
9. Who is recognised as a knower, and what types of knowledge are deemed valuable?
10. Who is the author of the research, and who is the subject?
11. How can we ensure that research findings are relevant and accessible to the communities they discuss? Who is responsible for broadening the impact of research knowledge?

Engaging wider audiences: embracing a decolonial approach

Colonial systems relegated women and the colonised as not having reason (Ramose, 1999) – in other words as not being able to think, understand and form logical judgements. This perspective makes the call by Cutts (2020) – a Black and queer woman – for writing poetry in research as a way to fulfil a critical spiritual necessity to *(re)member* what colonialism tried to erase and annihilate particularly compelling. This historical context compels us to examine whether these biases continue to influence modern research practices, possibly leading to methodologies and writings that exclude or marginalise non-White and non-male perspectives. Kakali Bhattacharya (2019) advocates for viewing research subjects as knowledgeable agents who offer wisdom if they so choose. This approach requires rethinking our interactions with research participants, treating them as having the autonomy to decide how their knowledge is shared and the right to access and critique the resulting research. This paradigm shift is crucial for adopting a decolonial approach to research. It is in line with Ndlovu-Gatsheni's (2017) call to confront and rectify research's 'dirty history'.

Furthermore, Kessi et al (2020, p 271) define decolonisation as 'a political and normative ethic and practice of resistance and intentional undoing – unlearning and dismantling unjust practices, assumptions, and institutions – as well as persistent positive action to create and build alternative spaces, networks and ways of knowing that transcend our epi-colonial inheritance'.

This chapter focuses on *dismantling these unjust practices* in our research methodologies and *creating alternative spaces* in how we write and publish research, to ensure that our work is accessible and accountable to those it represents and affects (as illustrated in Figure 5.3).

Considering the audience is crucial, especially when adopting a decolonial approach to research. Traditional methods often exclude the very populations they study, with research predominantly published in European languages and academic formats that cater mainly to the Global North, often behind paywalls. This practice effectively bars those in the Global South, who are frequently the subjects of research, from accessing and

Figure 5.3: Embracing a decolonial approach

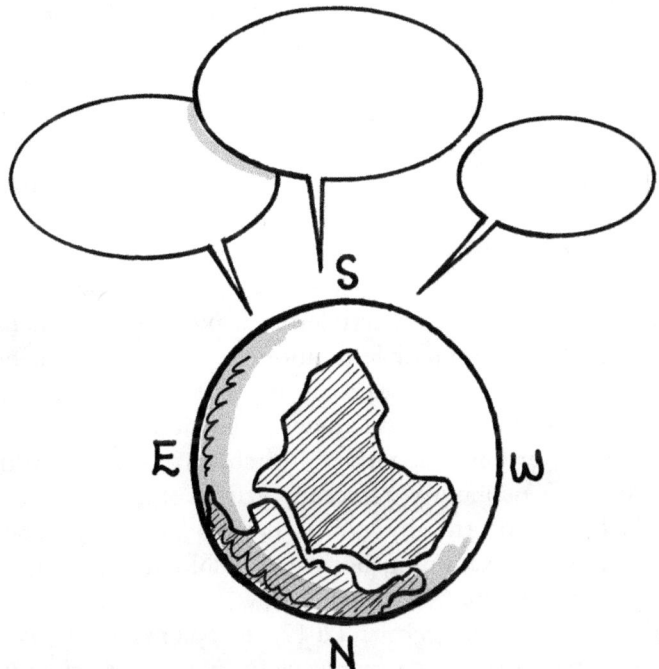

critically engaging with the work. Research is also typically conveyed in dense jargon, making it inaccessible to non-experts and reinforcing exclusivity. Despite a growing recognition of the value of subjectivity, research texts often remain devoid of emotion, ambiguity and contradiction – qualities that poetry can capture. Poetic inquiry, therefore, has the potential to broaden the reach of research, making it resonate more deeply with diverse audiences. However, without careful reflection on how we use poetic inquiry, we risk creating works that are still only accessible to a privileged few.

It is crucial to consider the intended audience when starting to design research. Research methods should be tailored to who will ultimately engage with the research output, as emphasised by Leavy (2017) and Patton (1990), who both advocate that the research audience should significantly influence the methodology used. This approach ensures that methodological decisions are inclusive and relevant to those who will interact with the findings. Although poetic inquiry may be incorporated at any stage, pre-emptively considering the audience can greatly enhance the research's impact.

Adopting a decolonial framework compels us to scrutinise how power dynamics within the research process can affect this consideration. The concept of the researcher as an instrument provides a valuable perspective on these dynamics. This concept emphasises that researchers bring diverse personal histories, knowledge and unique worldviews to the research process, all of which significantly shape their research identity (see Manathunga et al, 2019). These multiple positionings inevitably influence the dynamics between researchers and participants, impacting the power relations within these interactions. By focusing on how power operates within research, an evaluation of the quality of poetic inquiry transcends analysis of the final poetic products. It also critically assesses the process that generates these outputs, examining both methodological rigour and ethical considerations.

Historically, as Bhattacharya (2019) and Ramose (1999) note, certain groups have been marginalised in academic discourse and have often been perceived as lacking reason or agency. It is important to re-evaluate how researchers interact with participants and advocate for a more equitable partnership where participants are recognised as co-contributors of knowledge. In typical research settings, the researcher, often seen as the primary knower due to formal training, typically dictates research questions and controls the narrative output. This dynamic can marginalise other forms of knowledge, such as arts-based insights.

Poetic inquiry challenges these norms by facilitating a more inclusive approach where knowledge creation is collaborative. In this, researchers and participants co-create, allowing participants to assert their agency as knowers. This method not only democratises the research process but also makes the findings more accessible and engaging to a broader audience beyond the usual academic circles. By integrating poetic inquiry, the research output transcends conventional academic texts, reaches wider communities and fosters a richer, more diverse discourse.

Exercise: reflections on decoloniality and poetic inquiry

As you reflect on the transformative potential of poetic inquiry within a decolonial framework, consider the following points made by from key scholars:

- Bagele Chilisa (2019) highlights that research involves a power struggle, with researchers often defining, categorising and even prescribing what is needed by those they study. This places immense power in the hands of researchers to shape narratives and outcomes.
- Lincoln (2010) advocates for qualitative research to lead to positive social transformations and contribute towards creating a more just world.
- Pedri-Spade (2016, p 390) emphasises that 'doing good work' calls for a commitment to decolonising both our minds and our bodies, and suggests this is a holistic process.

Reflect on these points and consider how your understanding of poetic inquiry as decolonial praxis might enrich or challenge these perspectives.

- What insights or additional thoughts would you add to those points, based on your understanding of poetic inquiry as a decolonial tool? Consider how poetic inquiry can uniquely contribute to the power dynamics in research, social transformation and the decolonisation process.
- Reflect on the power dynamics involved in your research process. Who holds the power in determining the research focus, the questions asked and the outcomes pursued? How does this power influence the knowledge that is produced?
- Write a short reflection on how you could alter these dynamics to foster a more equitable relationship between

you as the researcher and the research participants. How could poetic inquiry support these goals?

- How have your views on decolonial research and poetic inquiry evolved throughout this book? Write a short paragraph reflecting on any shifts in your perspective or new insights you have gained.

- After writing down your reflections, consider how these insights might influence your future research practices.

Who do we write for? Understanding our audience

One of the best pieces of advice Duduzile S. Ndlovu (one of the authors of this chapter) received about writing research was: If you could read this to your grandmother, would she understand what you are saying? This question highlights the significant impact that the intended audience has on what we write and how we write it.

Exercise: tailoring your message for different audiences

In this exercise, you will explore how to communicate your research to various audiences. This will help you understand the flexibility required in presentation, and the importance of considering who your readers are.

1. Choose audiences

Select two or three audiences from the list that follows, and prepare to write a short paragraph about your research for each:
- a former high school friend who does not have a university degree
- a public transport operator (for example, a taxi or bus driver)
- a neighbour who is an engineer
- a high school class (ages 15–18)

- your parents and their friends
- a cashier at your local supermarket
- the leader of your country
- a spiritual leader (such as a pastor, imam or priest)
- peers in your research methods course
- your research supervisor
- the organisers of a conference on poetic inquiry

2. Write

Set a timer for up to three minutes and write a paragraph for each selected audience. Repeat this for each audience you have chosen.

3. Compare and reflect

- After writing, compare the paragraphs. Note any differences in language, tone and content. Reflect on why these changes occurred and what stayed the same across different versions.
- Consider how the necessity to shift your presentation style might relate to the underlying themes of your research and its reception.

4. Write a poem

Finally, set your timer for three minutes and write freely about your reflections on this exercise. Use this piece to craft a poem about how you consider different audiences when writing about your research.

5. Discussion points

- Reflect on how power dynamics influenced your decisions when tailoring your research presentation for different audiences.

- Explore whether you identified any potential to disrupt these power dynamics through the way you communicate your research.

In the next exercise, we consider an interaction between a researcher, Sabelo, and a research participant, Mthokozisi. This exercise will help you to think critically about the ethical dimensions of research. It will also help you explore the potential for poetic inquiry to disrupt typical power dynamics, enhance participant involvement and broaden the impact of research findings. Read the case study on the interaction between Sabelo and Mthokozisi before moving on to the exercise.

Case study: Sabelo and Mthokozisi

Sabelo: Hi my name is Sabelo, I am a researcher at the university of Utopia. Thank you for agreeing to meet with me.

Mthokozisi: Oh, hello, I was happy to get your request to meet. There is so much going on in our community.

Sabelo: Yes, I am doing research on water supply, and I would like to interview you about the recent water shortages in your area.

Mthokozisi: Oh yes, that has been going on for a quite a while. I've done so many interviews about it too, but no one ever bothers to send me what they write. I'm happy to talk to you about our situation.

Sabelo: [Talks about the purpose of the research and what consenting to the research means] Okay, I have this form which you will need to sign to show that you understand what participating in the interview means. Then we can start the interview.

Mthokozisi: Oh, I will gladly sign. Like I said I am happy to talk about the water problems in our area. I hope you won't disappear like the other people who have interviewed me. I never got to know what they wrote afterwards.

> Mthokozisi signs the consent form and gives Sabelo the interview he asked for. Sabelo leaves the interview and is happy he has a consent form that shows he asked for informed consent as outlined in his ethics approval.

Exercise: analysing outcomes and reflecting on decolonial ethics

1. Case study reflection

Write a short paragraph on two possible outcomes from the case study on Sabelo and Mthokozisi:

- **Outcome 1:** Sabelo follows traditional research protocols and publishes a widely cited journal article without further engaging with his participants.

- **Outcome 2:** Sabelo sends a copy of his published article to Mthokozisi as a form of feedback and acknowledgment.

2. Power dynamics

- Reflect on how power functions in each of the described outcomes. Consider who benefits from each outcome. How are the participants being treated in each scenario?

- Write a paragraph discussing the power dynamics and how they reflect traditional or decolonial research ethics.

3. Decolonial ethics reflection

- Discuss the importance of seeking an outcome beyond the first two, especially in the context of decolonising research. What would a truly decolonial approach look like in this scenario?

- Consider how changing the way we view and interact with research participants reflects a decolonial ethic. Write a few sentences on this topic.

4. Role of poetry in research

- Explore how poetry can be used to include research participants more integrally in the research process and in its outputs. What unique advantages does poetic inquiry offer in terms of participant engagement and expanding the audience for research?

- Write a short poem or creative piece that illustrates how poetry can bridge the gap between researchers and participants, potentially transforming the research dynamic.

5. Sharing and expanding the audience:

- Reflect on the benefits of including participants in the written outputs of your research. How does this practice enhance the research process and outcomes?

- Discuss ways in which poetry can help to expand the audience for your research. What are some strategies you could employ to make your research accessible and engaging for a broader audience, including those outside the academic community?

Return to the beginning

Reflect on your answer to the question posed earlier, about whether anyone can write poetry for research. Revisit your early stance in light of this chapter's discussion on poetic inquiry's quality and audience engagement. How have the insights on necessary skills, audience consideration and power dynamics influenced your views? Update your response, considering the importance of mastering both poetic craft and research methodologies. Think about how a decolonial approach and understanding audience dynamics shape who is best suited to undertake poetic inquiry.

Conclusion

This chapter emphasises the need to engage thoughtfully with both the craft of poetry and the ethics of research, ensuring that poetic inquiry satisfies artistic and scientific standards. We explored the principles of poetic inquiry as an arts-based, qualitative method, focusing on the importance of thinking qualitatively and being aware of researcher positionality to evaluate its scientific merit. We highlighted that while poetic inquiry need not produce award-winning poems, attention to craft is crucial. Not all poetry is meant for external audiences; some serve as a reflective tool for researchers to process emotions and experiences. Finally, we explored how a decolonial approach can reshape both the audience and conduct of research, challenging traditional power dynamics by enabling more diverse voices and communities to engage with and critique research in meaningful ways.

By focusing on quality evaluation and audience considerations, we aim to enhance the legitimacy and impact of poetic inquiry. This approach not only broadens the scope of audience engagement but also deepens the ethical dimensions of research, promoting a more inclusive and reflexive academic practice. The critical and creative integration of poetic inquiry within research methodologies has the transformative potential to revitalise academic discourse and contribute to a more equitable discourse in the research community and beyond.

Note

[1] eWallet is a system of sending and receiving cash via mobile telephones.

References

Barone, T. and Eisner, E.W. (2011) *Arts Based Research*, Los Angeles: Sage Publications.

Bhattacharya, K. (2019) 'Theorizing from the streets: de/colonizing, contemplative, and creative approaches and consideration of quality in arts-based qualitative research', in N.K. Denzin and M.D. Giardina (eds) *Qualitative Inquiry at a Crossroads: Political Performative and Methodological Reflections*, New York: Routledge, pp 109–25.

Chilisa, B. (2019) *Indigenous Research Methodologies*, Los Angeles: Sage Publications.

Cutts, Q.M. (2020) 'More than craft and criteria: the necessity of *ars spirituality* in (Black women's) poetic inquiry and research poetry', *Qualitative Inquiry*, 26(7): 908–19.

Faulkner, S.L. (2019) *Poetic Inquiry: Craft, Method and Practice*, New York: Routledge.

Finlay, L. (2006) '"Rigour", "ethical integrity" or "artistry"? Reflexively reviewing criteria for evaluating qualitative research', *British Journal of Occupational Therapy*, 69(7): 319–26.

Higgs, G.E. (2008) 'Psychology: knowing the self through arts', in J. Knowles and A. Cole (eds) *Handbook of the Arts in Qualitative Research: Perspectives, Methodologies, Examples, and Issues*, Los Angeles: Sage Publications, pp 545–57.

Kessi, S., Marks, Z. and Ramugondo, E. (2020) 'Decolonizing African studies', *Critical African Studies*, 12(3): 271–82.

Knowles, J.G. and Promislow, S. (2008) 'Using an arts methodology to create a thesis or dissertation', in J. Knowles and A. Cole (eds) *Handbook of the Arts in Qualitative Research: Perspectives, Methodologies, Examples, and Issues*, Los Angeles: Sage Publications, pp 511–26.

Leavy, P. (2017) *Research Design: Quantitative, Qualitative, Mixed Methods, Arts-Based, and Community-Based Participatory Research Approaches*, New York: Guilford Press.

Leggo, C. (2011) 'What is a poem good for? 14 possibilities', *Journal of Artistic and Creative Education*, 5(1): 32–58.

Lincoln, Y.S. (2010) '"What a long, strange trip it's been …": 25 years of qualitative and new paradigm research', *Qualitative Inquiry*, 16(1): 3–9.

Manathunga, C., Qi, J., Bunda, T. and Singh, M. (2019) 'Time mapping: charting transcultural and First Nations histories and geographies in doctoral education', *Discourse: Studies in the Cultural Politics of Education*, 42(2): 215–33.

Ndlovu, D.S. (2020) 'Decolonizing writing: situating insider-outsider researchers in writing about COVID-19', in H. Kara and S.-M. Khoo (eds) *Researching in the Age of COVID-19 Volume III: Creativity and Ethics*, Bristol: Policy Press, pp 29–38.

Ndlovu-Gatsheni, S. (2017) 'Decolonising research methodology must include undoing its dirty history', *Journal of Public Administration*, 52(S1): 186–8.

Palmary, I. (2005) 'The possibility of a reflexive gaze: the relevance of feminist debates on reflexivity, representation and situated knowledges for psychology', in P. Kiguwa and T. Scaeffer (eds) The Gender of Psychology, Cape Town: UCT Press, pp 29–44.

Patton, M.Q. (1990) *Qualitative Evaluation and Research Methods*, Los Angeles: Sage Publications.

Pedri-Spade, C. (2016) '"The drum is your document": decolonizing research through Anishinabe song and story', *International Review of Qualitative Research*, 9(4): 385–406.

Ramose, M.B. (1999) *African Philosophy through Ubuntu*, Harare: Mond Books.

Sparkes, A.C. (2020) 'Poetic representations, not-quite poetry and poemish: some methodological reflections', in E. Fitzpartick and K. Fitzpatrick (eds) *Poetry, Method and Education Research*, New York: Routledge, pp 41–50.

Swaminathan, R. and Mulvihill, T.M. (2018) *Teaching Qualitative Research: Strategies for Engaging Emerging Scholars*, New York: Guilford Publications.

Williams, A.L. (2023) 'Writing through pain: ars spirituality, the Black Atlantic, and the paradox of diasporic belongingness', *Qualitative Inquiry*. doi: 10.1177/10778004231176096

6

Conclusion

Raphael d'Abdon and Heidi van Rooyen

This book is designed to guide readers from all walks of life into a learning, transformative and generative experience; both the neophyte and the well-versed practitioner of poetic inquiry will benefit in many ways from what is offered in *Poetic Inquiry as Research: A Decolonial Guide*. As the title anticipates, the emphasis is placed not only on poetic inquiry as a research methodology, but also on its importance as an effective tool for lecturers, human and social scientists, poets, students and common readers interested in the decolonisation of curricula, syllabi, qualitative and quantitative research, daily practices or, even more ambitiously, the broader project of – to quote Ngũgĩ wa Thiong'o (1986) – the decolonisation of the mind.

In their 2020 article 'Transforming data into poems: poetic inquiry practices for social and human sciences', the editors of this book insist on anchoring the theory and practices of poetic inquiry to the concept of decolonisation. The 9th International Symposium on Poetic Inquiry, hosted by their research group in Cape Town in 2022, gave impetus to this 'new' (South) African approach, by interrogating the state and future of decolonial poetic inquiry on a global scale. The article and the symposium can now be seen as a preamble to this book, which represents a cohesive and sustained exploration of poetic inquiry not only as a decolonial method, but also as a 21st-century expression of African indigenous knowledge systems.

Chapter by chapter, this book unpacks the idea of poetic inquiry as a powerful decolonial methodology; as scholars writing from and operating in the Global South, we believe that this publication is not only a contribution to a field of study first imagined and then creatively developed in the Global North, but also a practical instrument to revive African epistemologies still largely forgotten, silenced and dismissed by 'Euro-Western' academia. Poetry is a tool that for millennia has shaped the very concept of science in the African continent: this book celebrates the wisdom encapsulated in this worldview and places poetry at the very centre of its decolonial narrative.

The activities contained here disrupt the more common approach taken to poetic inquiry; by using creative poetry activities as a way to think critically about research practices before, during and following 'traditional' data collection (rather than after the 'real' data has been collected, as a way to translate the insights for various audiences), this book sees poetry as a way into decolonial research and a way to reflexively engage with the social world as a researcher. Other proponents of poetic inquiry have outlined a similar exploratory (rather than translatory) approach, but this book highlights its significance as/for decolonial work.

The theoretical sections, the illustrative examples and the exercises aimed at perfecting the poetic craft point in the same direction: they expand conventional ways of mappings of knowledge, suggest liberating practices of reflexivity and self-expression, facilitate a 'humanistic' reorientation of life experiences and encourage a 'decolonising' exploration of identity through poetry. After reading this book and actively engaging with it, readers are empowered and equipped with multiple assets that can positively affect their performance in the classroom, in the workplace and in their everyday personal and relational endeavours: better knowledge of poetry and its healing, liberating power; fresh perspectives on how to do research in a fast-changing, de-Westernising world; and deeper understanding of power relations and one's role in both research and social environments.

The relations between Western and non-Western forms of knowledge are not binary: they have been in intimate interaction since the beginning of the colonial project, and in today's digital age they are more intertwined than ever; this book acknowledges in many ways this symbiotic relationship but suggests that contemporary representational processes such as poetic inquiry are needed in contexts in which decolonisation is seen as a priority. The concept of poetic inquiry has travelled, been transformed and been enthusiastically deployed the world over, and hopefully this book can be a valid contribution to the growth of this area of study.

Like the great decolonial thinker Frantz Fanon said: 'there is a point at which methods devour themselves' (1968, p 12). In recent years, more and more people working in academia and research spaces have shown disillusion and frustration towards academic jargon and the established methods of doing research. Certainly, each of the editors and contributors to this volume at some point in their life and professional journey shared these feelings and, in their search for new ways of doing research, found each other and the global poetic inquiry family. We hope that this book will represent an entry point to this fascinating community and a useful tool for readers in search of innovative, creative and empowering ways of doing research, whether oriented towards decolonial practices or not.

References

Fanon, F. (1968) *The Wretched of the Earth* (trans C. Farrington), Grove Press: New York.

Ngũgĩ wa Thiong'o (1986) *Decolonising the Mind: The Politics of Language in African Literature*, London: Heinemann Educational Books.

Index

References to figures appear in *italic* type; those in **bold** type refer to tables. References to endnotes show both the page number and the note number (121n3).

A

Afriku (African haiku) 41, **42**, 43
Agyei-Baah, Adjei 41
Akomolafe, Bayo 83
All About Love (hooks) 94
alliteration 66
Almudéver Chanzà, Josep 34, 85
anaphora 66
anonymity 121, 124, 148
anti-colonisation *see* decolonisation
Anzaldúa, Gloria 141–42
The Art of Waiting for Tales (Xaba) 96
arts-based research 158–59, 161–62, **162**
assonance 66, 68
audiences 83, **90**, 161–62, 166–67, 169–72, 174–76, 178–79
Australia 15, 86–87
auto-ethnography 99–100, 109
autonomy 120, 170

B

'Bad blood' (Sliep) 146–47
Ballantyne, C.T. 21–22
Barone, T. 161–62
'being coloured' (van Rooyen) 6–7
'Belonging begins in exile' (Hough) 142–43
Bene, Carmelo 93
beneficence *120*, 121, 151–52
Bhattacharya, Kakali 8, 13, 15, 23, 170, 172
Bintz, William P. 48
Boswell, Barbara 95–96
Brooks, Gwendolyn 48
Brown, Jericho 48
Brown, Nicole 3
Butler-Kisber, L. 92

C

cadence 67
'Can we be like water' (Layne) 54–55
Césaire, Aimé 10, 41
Chambers, L. 18, 38–39
Chilisa, Bagele 173
co-creation
  co-created poems 101, 136–37, 146–47
  poetic inquiry, as tool of 82, 84, 86, 100–101, 102, 103
cognitive injustices 14, 15
collaboration **16**, 19–20, 82, 84, 135–36, 161, 172
Collins, Patricia Hill 128–29
colonial histories 4–6
coloniality 4, 8
colonial research
  impacts of 18, 78, 141, 170
  methodologies 8, 10
  neutrality in 78, 80, 126
colonisation 4
concrete poems *see* shape poems (concrete poems)
consent *see* informed consent
context 78, 80, **89**, 121, 170
Crenshaw, Kimberlé 127
Crilly, J. 4
critical consciousness 21–22, 25
critical reflexivity *see* reflexivity
Cutts, Q.M. 166, 170

D

d'Abdon, Raphael 15, 38, **42**, 49, 84, 92–93, 96, 102–103, 110–11

Dalal, F. 82
Dark, Kimberly 3
data
  decolonial research and **16**, 17, 21, 88
  poetry, transforming into 92, 95, 99, 102–103, 110–111, 118, 184–85
  positionality and 119
  power dynamics and 127, 129–30
  thinking qualitatively 159, 160–61, 162
  validity of 121
Davis, C. 2
'Day three' (Ndlovu) xviii
Deane, Kirsten 44, 46, 59–60, 61, 63–64
'decoloniality' (van Rooyen) 9
decolonial research
  audiences 170–72, 174–76
  author's overview of 7–8, 17, 79–80
  critical consciousness 21–22, 25
  definitions of 9–10
  ethical considerations 119–22, 124–25, 151–52, 176–78
  indigenous worldviews 14–16, **16**
  listening 79, 80, *83*, 83–84, 121
  marginalised voices **16**, 16–18, 79, 135–38
  methodologies 17, 118
  participatory research **16**, 19–21
  principles of 14–22, **16**
  social justice 134–35
  see also co-creation; collaboration; data; exercises in this book; research poems
decolonisation
  definitions of 4, 170
  narratives, as challenging 14–15
  time-mapping 4–7, *5*
Decolonizing Methodologies (Smith) 8
Denzin, N.K. 112
Dutta, U. 12, 13

E

'Easter' (Yeats) 68
Eisner, E.W. 161–62
end rhyme 67
epistrophe 66
ethical research 119–22, 124–25, 151–52, 176–78
ethics of practice 124–25

evaluation of poetic inquiry 159–162, **162**, **165**, 165–66
Everitt, E. 4
exercises in this book
  audiences, tailoring message for 174–76
  decolonial manifesto 85
  decolonial research ethics 177–78
  decolonial research practices 10–11
  decolonial research principles 22–23
  figures of speech: metaphors 61–62
  figures of speech: personification 64
  figures of speech: similes 60
  poems, connecting with 36–37
  poems, developing generated 94–95
  poems, rhythm/rhyme/repetition 68–69
  poems, writing for research 157
  poetic forms: Afriku 43
  poetic forms: free verse 45
  poetic forms: ghazal 51–52
  poetic forms: golden shovel 49–50
  poetic forms: narrative poems 47–48
  poetic forms: pantoum 57–58, 140–41
  poetic inquiry, decolonising research through 81, 138
  poetic inquiry, defining and mapping 91
  poetic inquiry, discovering yourself 143–45
  poetic inquiry, evaluation of 165–66
  poetry, discovering definitions in 35–36
  poetry, exploring your relationship with 37
  reflections on messiness 23
  reflections on poetic inquiry 111–112, 173–74
  reflections on power dynamics 81, 123–24, 130–32, 132–34, 173–74
  time-mapping 6

F

Fanon, Frantz 4, 185
'Fathers and Sons' (Deane) 44, 59–60, 61
Faulkner, Sandra 110, 156, 158, 162, 164
feminists 129

Index

figures of speech
  author's overview of 58, *59*, 69–70
  imagery 64–65
  metaphors 60–62
  personification 63–64
  schemes 58, 65
  similes 59–60
  tropes 58, 65
Flecker, James Elroy 50–51
forms *see* poetic forms
foundational techniques of poetry
  author's overview of 65, **66**
  repetition 66, **66**, 68–69
  rhyme **66**, 67–68, 68–69
  rhythm **66**, 67, 68–69
'Found poem: Acceptance' (van Rooyen) 20–21
found poems/poetry
  author's overview of 48, 86, 92
  co-creation of 136–38
  decolonial research using 86–87
  development of, examples of 104–110
  golden shovel poetry 48–50
  as poetic inquiry 95–98
  voice types in 98–101
Francis (Saint) 77
free verse 44–45

G

Garuba, Harry 39
generated poems 92–95
ghazal 50–53, 70n4
Global North xvii, 17, 170–71
Global South xvii, 17–18, 157, 170–71, 184
golden shovel poetry 48–50
Grace (Boswell) 95–96
Gumede, Zonke 87
Gxwayibeni, Fezeka 3

H

haiku 41–43
half rhyme (imperfect rhyme) 68
Harding, Sandra 126
Hayes, Terrance 48
Henson, Lance 36, 70
Higgs, Johan 157
'Home' (Gumede and Makiwane) 87–88
hooks, bell 94, 129
Hough, Angela 107–109, 142–43
'How does it sit?' (Sliep) 149–50

I

'I am gay' (Kaunda and Fubah) 78–79
identity
  exploration of through poetry 12, 34, 76, 106
  poems on 78–79, 142–48
  of researchers 11, 19, 25, 80
  see also intersectionality
'I have no one' (van Rooyen) 104–105
imagery 64–65
indigenous research 17–18
indigenous ways of knowing
  colonialism on, impact of 18, 141
  decolonial research and 14–15, 16, 20, 21
  poetry and 37–38, 38–39
indigenous worldviews 14–16, **16**, 19
informed consent 120, 124, 148, 176–77
injustices 14, 15, 135
'In Taiwan' (Sliep) 99–100
internal rhyme 66, 67–68
International Symposium of Poetic Inquiry (ISPI) xvii–xviii, 3, 184
intersectionality
  author's overview of 127–29, *128*, 135
  poems on 3, 77, 98–99, 110
  of researchers 7, 11
  see also identity
invisibility 3, 17 *see also* marginalised communities
ISPI *see* International Symposium of Poetic Inquiry (ISPI)
'I will remember' (d'Abdon) 49

K

Kessi, S. 170
'Kiliba Village, East DRC' (Sliep) 56–57
'Kin' (Angelou) 49
knowledge production
  collaborative 161
  colonial research 7, 8, 14, 17, 18
  decolonial research 7–8, 14–16, 17, 19–21, 82
Knowles, J.G. 157, 161

L

'La bouteille' (Panard) *54*
'La verre' (Panard) *54*
Layne, Tanya 54–55
Leavy, P. 161, 171

Leggo, Carl 166
'Less of me' (Sliep) 130–31
liminal spaces 141–43
Lincoln, Y.S. 112, 173
listening 79, 80, 83, 83–84, 121
literature-voiced poems 98–99
'Little Pains' (Deane) 63–64
Lorde, Audre 39
'Lost' (Wagoner) 61–62

M

Makiwane, Monde 87
Maldonado-Torres, N. 4, 17
Manathunga, C. 4
'Manifesto of poetic inquiry' (Hough) 77–78
Maposa, Tamuka 3
marginalised communities
　participatory research with 19–21, 135–38
　voices of 15–18, **16**, 79–81, 135–38, 138–41
Mashigo, Mohale 95
Mehu, C.M. 21–22
metaphors 60–62
meter 67
Moletsane, R. 16
'Motherhood' (Hough) 107–109

N

Namibia 20, **106**, 106–107, 136–38
narrative poems 45–48
Ndlovu, Duduzile S. 174
Ndlovu, Malika (poet) xviii, 80–81, 167–68
Ndlovu-Gatsheni, S. 14, 170
Ngcongo, Sipho 146–48
'Nobody is safe' (van Rooyen) 136–37
Norton, Lynn 84–85

O

objectivity 126
'One month' (Sliep) 100
'Opening and anchoring' (Ndlovu) 80–81
oral traditions 38
othering 79, 80
'Own my life today' (Ndlovu) 122

P

pantoum 56–58, 138–41
participant-based poems 100–101

participants *see* research participants
participatory research **16**, 19–21, 134–35, 135–38
'Pass for white' (van Rooyen) 23–24
Patton, M.Q. 171
Pedri-Spade, C. 173
personification 63–64
perspectives
　colonial 7–8, 170
　decolonial 82–83, 159
　of researchers 7, 11, 76, 80, 126
　of research participants 14, 16–18, 19–21, 121, 141
　see also voices
Phakathi, V. 39–41
poems
　on colonisation impacts 18
　on decolonisation 9
　on family 44, 86–87
　on grief 99–100, 168
　on home 46, 86–87, 87–88
　on homelessness 104–105
　on identity 142–43, 145–46, 146–48
　on intersectional experiences 3, 20–21, 78–79
　on marginalised voices 15, 80–81
　on motherhood 107–109
　on poetic inquiry 77–78, 82–83, 84
　on power dynamics 122–23
　on reflexivity 139–40, 149–50, 168
　on skin colour 6–7, 23–24
　on trans experience 20–21, **106**, 136–37
poetic forms
　Afriku (African haiku) 41, **42**, 43
　author's overview of 43–44, 83–84
　free verse 44–45
　ghazal 50–53, 70n4
　golden shovel poetry 48–50
　haiku 41–43
　narrative poems 45–48
　pantoum 56–58, 138–41
　shape poems (concrete poems) 53–55, *54*, 71n5
poetic inquiry
　audiences 83, **90**, 161–62, 166–67, 169–72, 174–76, 178–79
　author's overview of xvii, 2–3, 79–80, 88–89
　benefits of 12–14, 82
　evaluation of 159–162, **162**, **165**, 165–66

generated poems 92–95
and liminal spaces 141–43
poems on 77–78, 82–83, 84
quality of 157–59
and social change 134–35
see also co-creation; collaboration; decolonial research; exercises in this book; found poems/poetry; research poems
Poetic Inquiry for the Human and Social Sciences (van Rooyen and Pithouse-Morgan) 3
poetry
in Africa 38–39
author's overview of 34, 85–86
definitions of 34, 35–36
poetic inquiry, compared 89, **89–90**
slam poetry 15, 96–98
in South Africa 39–41
see also figures of speech; foundational techniques of poetry; found poems/poetry; poetic forms
positionality 80, 119, 130–32, 146–48, 159
power
colonial systems of 4, 79
data and 127, 129–30
power dynamics in research 9–10, 118, 119–124, 130–34, 172
reflexivity and 15–16, **16**, 25, 125–26, 141
Prendergast, M. 98, 101
privileging
and power 132–34
of skin colour 23–24
of worldviews 14
procedural ethics 124
Promislow, S. 157, 161

Q

qualitative research 2, 76, 102, 119–21, *120*, 158–59
qualitative thinking 159–62
quality of poetic inquiry 157–59
see also evaluation of poetic inquiry

R

Ramose, M.B. 172
'Re-authoring' (Ngcongo) 147–48
reflexive poetry 167–69

reflexivity
author's overview of 141
decolonial research and 15–16, **16**, 125–26
development of by researchers 129–30, 132, 141–46, 146–49, 151
poems on 139–40
repetition 66, **66**, 68–69
research *see* arts-based research; colonial research; data; decolonial research; ethical research; participatory research; qualitative research; researchers; research participants
researchers
identity of 11, 19, 25, 80
intersectionality of 7, 11
perspectives of 7, 11, 76, 80, 126
poetic skills of 162–64, **165**
qualitative thinking 159–62
reflexive poetry by 167–69
voices of 82
see also reflexivity
researcher-voiced poems 99–100
research participants
anonymity of 121, 124, 148
autonomy of 120, 170
informed consent 120, 124, 148, 176–77
voices of 79
see also co-creation; collaboration; participatory research
research poems
data into, transforming 92, 95, 99, 102–103, 110–111, 118, 184–85
guidelines for creating 102–103
stand-alone poems, compared 89, **89–90**
voices in 98–101
rhyme 66, 67–68, 68–69
rhythm 66, 67, 68–69
rigour 118, 120–22, 126, 127, 159

S

schemes 58, 65
Shahrazad 38
'shakespeare didn't work for me' (d'Abdon) 93–94
shape poems (concrete poems) 53–55, *54*, 71n5
similes 59–60
slam poetry 15, 96–98
Sliep, Yvonne 56, 89, 99–101, 129–30, 139–40, 146

Smallwood, R. 15
Smith, Linda Tuhiwai 8
social change 134–35
social injustices 135
social justice 56–57, 134–35
South Africa
   International Symposium of Poetic Inquiry xvii, 184
   languages 39, 70n1
   participatory research in 20
   poems about/from xviii, 3, 87–88, 104–105
   poetry in 39–41
   Shakespeare in 93–94
   time-mapping 4–6, 5
   writers from 14–15, 95–96
Sparkes, Andrew 158
Spivak, Gayatri Chakravorty 129
subjectivity 7, 126, 171
Szymborska, Wisława 70

T

'The light' (Harris) 145–46
'The Poet' (Hough) 82–83
'This is fine' (Smallwood) 15
'This world' (Ndlovu) 167–68
The Thousand and One Nights (Eliot) 38
time-mapping 4–7, 5
Timothy, Alexander 18
'to slam or not to slam?' (d'Abdon) 96–98
traditional research *see* colonial research
'Transforming Data into poems' (van Rooyen and d'Abdon) 184
trans women 20–21, **106**, 106–107, 136–38
tropes 58, 65
trustworthiness 126–27, 159

U

'Unsilencing my teaching voice' (Timothy) 18

V

validity 121, 156, 159
van Rooyen, Heidi 4–7, 12–13, 20, 23–24, 38, 84, 98–99, 102–103, 110–11, 136
voices
   marginalised 15–18, **16**, 79–81, 135–38, 138–41
   oral traditions 38
   poetic, developing 163–64
   of researchers 82
   of research participants 79
   in research poems 98–101
   see also perspectives
vox autobiographia/autoethnographia 99–100
vox participare 100–101
vox theoria 98–99

W

'walking the talk is a lifelong process' (Sliep) 139–40
ways of knowing, indigenous 14–15, 20, 38–39, 141
'What you need' (Deane) 46
'Whitewash' (Brown) 3
Whose Science? (Harding) 126
Williams, A.L. 166
worldviews 14–16, **16**, 19

X

Xaba, Makhosazana 95–96

Y

'Yasmin' (Flecker) 50–51
'Yearning' (Xaba) 96
The Yearning (Mashigo) 95
'You could scream the place down' (Joy) 86–87

Z

Zavala, M. 19

www.ingramcontent.com/pod-product-compliance
Lightning Source LLC
Chambersburg PA
CBHW051542020426
42333CB00016B/2063